Level 2

BENCHMARK SERIES

Microsoft®

Word

365

2019 Edition

Review and Assessment

Nita Rutkosky | **Audrey Roggenkamp**
Pierce College Puyallup
Puyallup, Washington

Ian Rutkosky
Pierce College Puyallup
Puyallup, Washington

PARADIGM
EDUCATION SOLUTIONS

St. Paul

Vice President, Content and Digital Solutions: Christine Hurney
Director of Content Development: Carley Fruzzetti
Developmental Editor: Jennifer Joline Anderson
Director of Production: Timothy W. Larson
Production Editor/Project Manager: Jen Weaverling
Senior Design and Production Specialist: Jack Ross
Cover and Interior Design: Valerie King
Copy Editor: Communicáto, Ltd.
Testers: Janet Blum, Traci Post
Indexer: Terry Casey
Vice President, Director of Digital Products: Chuck Bratton
Digital Projects Manager: Tom Modl
Digital Solutions Manager: Gerry Yumul
Senior Director of Digital Products and Onboarding: Christopher Johnson
Supervisor of Digital Products and Onboarding: Ryan Isdahl
Vice President, Marketing: Lara Weber McLellan
Marketing and Communications Manager: Selena Hicks

Care has been taken to verify the accuracy of information presented in this book. However, the authors, editors, and publisher cannot accept responsibility for web, email, newsgroup, or chat room subject matter or content, or for consequences from the application of the information in this book, and make no warranty, expressed or implied, with respect to its content.

Trademarks: Microsoft is a trademark or registered trademark of Microsoft Corporation in the United States and/or other countries. Some of the product names and company names included in this book have been used for identification purposes only and may be trademarks or registered trade names of their respective manufacturers and sellers. The authors, editors, and publisher disclaim any affiliation, association, or connection with, or sponsorship or endorsement by, such owners.

Paradigm Education Solutions is independent from Microsoft Corporation and not affiliated with Microsoft in any manner.

Cover Photo Credit: © lowball-jack/GettyImages

We have made every effort to trace the ownership of all copyrighted material and to secure permission from copyright holders. In the event of any question arising as to the use of any material, we will be pleased to make the necessary corrections in future printings.

ISBN 978-0-76388-719-3 (print)
ISBN 978-0-76388-708-7 (digital)

© 2020 by Paradigm Publishing, LLC
875 Montreal Way
St. Paul, MN 55102
Email: CustomerService@ParadigmEducation.com
Website: ParadigmEducation.com

Printed in the United States of America

28 27 26 25 24 23 22 21 20 19   1 2 3 4 5 6 7 8 9 10 11 12

Contents

Microsoft® Word Level 2

Unit 1

Formatting and Customizing Documents

Microsoft® Word
Review and Assessment

CHAPTER

1

Applying Advanced Formatting

 The online course includes additional review and assessment resources.

Skills Assessment

Assessment

1

Apply Character Spacing and OpenType Features to a Donations Document

1. Open **PRDonations** and then save it with the name **1-PRDonations**.
2. Select the quote text *"In every community there is work to be done. In every nation there are wounds to heal. In every heart there is the power to do it."* and then apply stylistic set 4. (Do this at the Font dialog box with the Advanced tab selected.)
3. Select the heading *Domestic Donations* and change the scale to 90% and the spacing to Expanded. (Do this at the Font dialog box with the Advanced tab selected.)
4. Apply the same formatting in Step 3 to the heading *International Donations*.
5. Select the numbers in the *Domestic Donations* section. **Hint: To select only the numbers, position the mouse pointer at the beginning of $450,000, press and hold down the Alt key, use the mouse pointer to drag down and select the four numbers in the second column, and then release the Alt key.**
6. With the numbers selected, change the number spacing to Tabular spacing. (Do this at the Font dialog box with the Advanced tab selected.)
7. Select the numbers in the *International Donations* section and then change the number spacing to Tabular spacing.
8. Select the text *We are dedicated to working toward a more just and peaceful world.* and then insert a check mark in the *Use Contextual Alternates* check box at the Font dialog box with the Advanced tab selected.
9. Save, print, and then close **1-PRDonations**.

Assessment

2

Find and Replace Formatting and Use a Wildcard Character in an Employee Guide Document

1. Open **EmpGuide** and then save it with the name **1-EmpGuide**.
2. Find text set in the +Headings font and replace the font with Candara.
3. Find text set in the +Body font and replace the font with Constantia.
4. Find text set in 11-point Candara and replace it with 12-point Candara italic.
5. Using a wildcard charcter, find all occurrences of *Ne?land?Davis* and replace them with *Newland-Davis*.
6. Select the title *Newland-Davis Medical* and then change the scale option to 150% and the spacing option to Expanded. (Do this at the Font dialog box with the Advanced tab selected.)
7. Save, print, and then close **1-EmpGuide**.

3

Replace Special Characters, Insert Document Properties, and Inspect and Check the Accessibility of a First Aid Training Flyer

1. Open **FirstAidTraining** and then save it with the name **1-FirstAidTraining**.
2. Move the insertion point immediately right of *Health* in the subtitle *Sponsored by Frontline Health* and then insert a trademark symbol.
3. Search for all occurrences of hyphens and replace them with nonbreaking hyphens.
4. Search for all occurrences of em dashes and replace them with en dashes.
5. Display the Info backstage area and then type First Aid Training in the *Title* document property text box.
6. Display the 1-FirstAidTraining Properties dialog box and then type the following in each specified document property:
   a. Subject: Training
   b. Company: Tri-State Products
   c. Keywords: first aid, training, CPR
7. Save the document and then inspect the document and remove headers, footers, and watermarks.
8. Complete an accessibility check and then insert alternate text for the picture image by typing Stethoscope image in the text box in the Alt Text task pane. Position the picture image inline with text and then close all open task panes.
9. Print only the document properties.
10. Save, print, and then close **1-FirstAidTraining**.

Check a Travel Document for Accessibility Issues

1. Open **TTSAdventures** and then save it with the name **1-TTSAdventures**.
2. Using the Help feature, learn more about the rules for the Accessibility Checker.
3. After reading the information, complete an accessibility check on the document. Look at the errors that appear in the Accessibility Checker task pane and then correct each error.
4. Save, print, and then close **1-TTSAdventures**.
5. Open a blank document and then type text explaining the errors that were found in **1-TTSAdventures** by the Accessibility Checker and what you did to correct the errors.
6. Save the completed document and name it **1-TTSAccessibility**.
7. Print and then close **1-TTSAccessibility**.

Visual Benchmark

Format a Travel Document

1. Open **Hawaii** and then save it with the name **1-Hawaii**.
2. Apply the following formatting so your document appears similar to the document shown in Figure 1.1:
   - Inspect the document and remove the watermark (the watermark is in the footer) and the header.
   - Expand the spacing (by increasing the spacing point size) for the title and apply a stylistic set so your title appears similar to the title in the figure.
   - Expand the spacing (by increasing the spacing point size) and apply a stylistic set to the two headings in the document so the headings appear similar to the headings in the figure.

- Apply a stylistic set to the quote and the author of the quote near the bottom of the page.
- Select the tabbed text and then use the Text Effects and Typography button in the Font group on the Home tab to apply the tabular lining number style.
- Search for all occurrences of em dashes and replace each with a colon followed by a space.
- Search for all occurrences of hyphens and replace each with an en dash.
- Insert the trademark symbol as shown in the figure.

3. Save, print, and then close **1-Hawaii**.

Figure 1.1 Visual Benchmark

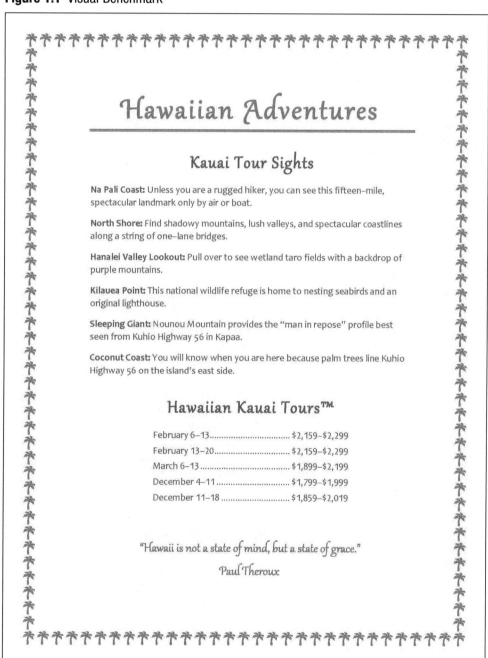

Case Study

Part 1

You are the assistant to the executive director of Phoenix Rising, a nonprofit organization. Phoenix Rising is sponsoring an affordable housing forum and you need to format a flyer for the event. Open **PRForum** and then save it with the name **1-PRForum**. The information about the forum is provided in the document and your responsibility is to apply attractive and appealing formatting to the information. To provide a frame of reference for formatting, open **1-PRDonations** and **1-PRDonorApp** to see how those documents are formatted and then apply similar formatting to **1-PRForum**. Replace any regular hyphens with en dashes and consider whether you want to have an em dash or other punctuation after *Date*, *Time*, and *Location*. Save, print, and then close **1-PRForum**.

Part 2

The executive director of Phoenix Rising needs a new organizational chart. Open **PRLtrhd** and then save it with the name **1-PROrgChart**. Look at the information in Figure 1.2 below and then create a SmartArt organizational chart to display the information. Provide a title for the organizational chart and apply formatting so the title and organizational chart appear similar to the other documents you prepared in this case study. Save, print, and then close **1-PROrgChart**.

Figure 1.2 Case Study, Part 2

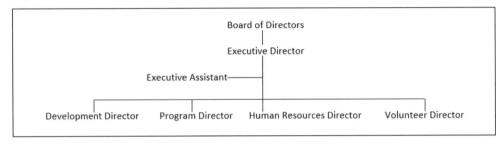

Part 3

The executive director wants to ensure that all documents you prepare for Phoenix Rising are checked for accessibility issues and has asked you to check two documents. Open **1-PRForum**, run an accessibility check on the document, and fix any errors identified by the Accessibility Checker. Save and then close **1-PRForum**. Open **1-PROrgChart**, run an accessibility check, and fix any errors identified by the Accessibility Checker. Save and then close **1-PROrgChart**. Open **PRLtrhd** and then save it with the name **1-PRAccessibility**. Write a letter to the executive director explaining any accessibility issues found in each document by the Accessibility Checker and the steps you took to correct them. Save, print, and then close **1-PRAccessibility**.

Part 4

To further identify a document and its contents, the executive director has asked you to provide document properties for **1-PROrgChart**. Open **1-PROrgChart** and then insert at least the following document properties:

- Title
- Author (use your name)
- Company
- Keywords

After inserting the document properties, save **1-PROrgChart**, print only the document properties, and then close the document.

CHAPTER
2

Proofing Documents

 The online course includes additional review and assessment resources.

Skills Assessment

Assessment 1

Check Spelling in a Document

1. Open **QuoteMarks** and then save it with the name **2-QuoteMarks**.
2. Complete a spelling and grammar check on the document.
3. Apply the Heading 1 style to the title of the document and the Heading 2 style to the headings in the document (which currently display with bold formatting).
4. Apply the Parallax theme.
5. Center the document title.
6. Save, print, and then close **2-QuoteMarks**.

Assessment 2

Check Spelling and Grammar and Proofread a Letter

1. Open **AirMiles** and then save it with the name **2-AirMiles**.
2. Complete a spelling and grammar check on the document. (Proper names are spelled correctly.)
3. After completing the spelling and grammar check, proofread the letter and make any necessary changes. (The letter contains mistakes that the grammar checker will not select.) Replace the *XX* near the end of the document with your initials.
4. Select the entire document and then change the font to 12-point Candara.
5. Save, print, and then close **2-AirMiles**.

Assessment 3

Check Spelling and Grammar and Display Readability Statistics and Word Count in a Document

1. Open **Ethics** and then save it with the name **2-Ethics**.
2. Turn on the display of readability statistics and then complete a spelling and grammar check on the document.
3. Make a note of the Flesch Reading Ease score and the Flesch-Kincaid Grade Level score and then type that information in the appropriate locations at the end of the document.
4. Turn off the display of readability statistics.
5. Determine the number of words in the document and then type that information in the appropriate location at the end of the document.
6. Insert continuous line numbering.
7. Apply formatting to enhance the appearance of the document.
8. Save, print, and then close **2-Ethics**.

Assessment
4

Translate Selected Text in a Document

1. Open **PRConference** and then save it with the name **2-PRConference**.
2. Select all the text in the first cell in the table (begins with *Annual Conference*).
3. Display the Translator task pane with the *Selection* option selected.
4. Specify that the text is to be translated into Spanish.
5. Click in the empty row at the bottom of the table and then insert the translated text.
6. Close the Translator task pane.
7. Save, print, and then close **2-PRConference**.

Assessment
5

Translate an Entire Document

1. Open **Announcement** and then save it with the name **2-Announcement**.
2. Translate the entire document into French.
3. Save the translated document and name it **2-Announce-French**.
4. Print and then close **2-Announce-French**.
5. Close the Translator task pane and then close **2-Announcement**.

Assessment
6

Sort Text in a Document

1. Open **SFSSorting** and then save it with the name **2-SFSSorting**.
2. Select the nine lines of text below the heading *Executive Team* and then sort the text alphabetically by last name.
3. Sort the three columns of text below the title *New Employees* by date of hire in ascending order.
4. Sort the text in the *First Qtr.* column in the table numerically in descending order.
5. Save, print, and then close **2-SFSSorting**.

Visual Benchmark

Activity
1

Sort Data in a Document

1. Open **Natura** and then save it with the name **2-Natura**.
2. Complete sorts so your text appears as shown in Figure 2.1. ***Hint: Sort the text in the table first by the country and then by the customer name***.
3. Save, print, and then close **2-Natura**.

Activity
2

Translate Text

1. Open **CCDonations** and then save it with the name **2-CCDonations**.
2. Type the paragraph of text below the heading *English:* as shown in Figure 2.2 on page 10 and then complete a spelling and grammar check on the text.
3. Select the paragraph of text below the heading *English:* and then translate the paragraph into Spanish and then into French. Insert the translated text into the document, as shown in Figure 2.2 (Your translations may vary from those shown in the figure.)
4. Use the Curlz MT font to format the heading at the beginning of each paragraph and the quote that displays near the end of the letter. Center the quote and apply the Blue font color to the quote and then apply paragraph shading as shown in the figure.
5. Save, print, and then close **2-CCDonations**.

Figure 2.1 Visual Benchmark 1

Natura
Natural products for natural beauty…

Natura Representatives

Denise Beaulieu	206-555-3901
Marcus Brown	347-555-2389
Charles Collins	202-555-9954
Dallas Conway	305-555-3492
Midori Fujita	504-555-7384
Isaac Hill	520-555-4366
Finn McDougal	312-444-0394
Paulina Menzel	346-555-2348
Hamilton Pierce	410-555-2384
Genevieve Salinger	602-555-4392

Natura Customers

Customer	Street Address	City	State/ Province	Postal Code	Country
Flying Queen	478 River Ave.	Winnipeg	MB	V4B 4A9	Canada
Rose	467 Seventh St. E.	Saskatoon	SK	S7H1A3	Canada
Swan	347 Park St.	Halifax	NS	B3H 2W2	Canada
Wave Rider	342 W. Georgia	Vancouver	BC	V6E 3H7	Canada
Beauty	89 Kiefer Creek Rd.	Ballwin	MO	63021	USA
Belle	P.O. Box 359	Belt	MT	59412	USA
Blue Fairy	307 Gold Hill Dr.	Grass Valley	CA	95945	USA
Maiden	345 Polk St.	San Francisco	CA	94109	USA
Melody	P.O. Box 789	Stromsburg	NE	68666	USA
Nautilus	45 Scarborough St.	Hartford	CT	06105	USA
Nina's Gift	784 Arizona Ave.	Santa Monica	CA	90401	USA
Red Coral	67 N. 73rd St.	Omaha	NE	68114	USA
Sailing Beauty	358 Fifth Ave.	Anchorage	AK	99501	USA
Sea Princess	876 N. Roxboro St.	Durham	NC	27701	USA
Suzanna	2331 S. Pioneer St.	Abilene	TX	79605	USA
The Dolphin	478 Dodson Dr.	East Point	GA	30344	USA
The Mermaid	782 West Fairway Pl.	Chandler	AZ	85224	USA
The Picasso	784 Parks St.	Duxbury	MA	02331	USA
Water Spirit	215 Vine St.	Cincinnati	OH	45202	USA
Woodwinds	34 Downey Ave.	Modesto	CA	95354	USA

Figure 2.2 Visual Benchmark 2

Cordova Children's Community Center

Support Your Local Community Center

English:

As you consider your donation contributions for the coming year, we ask that you consider your community by supporting the Cordova Children's Community Center. The center is a nonprofit agency providing educational and recreational activities for children. Please stop by for a visit. Our dedicated staff will be available to discuss with you the services offered by the center, how your donation dollars are spent, and provide information on current and future activities and services.

Spanish:

Al considerar sus contribuciones de donación para el próximo año, le pedimos que considere a su comunidad apoyando el Cordova Children's Community Center. El centro es una agencia sin fines de lucro que ofrece actividades educativas y recreativas para los niños. Por favor, visítanos. Nuestro personal dedicado estará disponible para discutir con usted los servicios ofrecidos por el centro, cómo se gastan sus dólares de donación, y proporcionar información sobre las actividades y servicios actuales y futuros.

French:

Comme vous considérez vos contributions de don pour l'année à venir, nous vous demandons de considérer votre communauté en soutenant le centre communautaire des enfants de Cordova. Le centre est une Agence à but non lucratif offrant des activités éducatives et récréatives pour les enfants. Veuillez vous arrêter pour une visite. Notre personnel dévoué sera disponible pour discuter avec vous des services offerts par le centre, comment vos dollars de Don sont dépensés, et fournir des informations sur les activités et les services actuels et futurs.

"Children are our most valuable natural resource." ~ Herbert Hoover

770 Sunrise Terrace ♦ Santa Fe, NM 87509 ♦ 505-555-7700

Case Study

Part
1

You work in the executive offices at Nickell Industries and have been asked to develop a writing manual for employees. The company has not used a consistent theme when formatting documents, so you decide to choose a theme and use it when formatting all Nickell documents. Open **NIManual** and then save the document and name it **2-NIManual**. Check the spelling and grammar in the document and then make the following changes to it:

- Insert a section break at the beginning of the title *Editing and Proofreading*.
- Apply styles of your choosing to the titles and headings in the document.
- Apply the theme you have chosen for company documents.
- Insert headers and/or footers.
- Create a cover page.
- Save the document.

Part
2

As you review the writing manual document you have created for Nickell Industries, you decide to highlight the points for developing sections of documents. You decide that a vertical block list SmartArt graphic will present the ideas in an easy-to-read format and provide some visual interest to the manual. Insert a page break at the end of the text in **2-NIManual**, type the title *Developing a Document*, and then insert the following in the appropriate shapes:

Beginning
- Introduce main idea.
- Get reader's attention.
- Establish a positive tone.

Middle
- Provide detail for main idea.
- Lead reader to intended conclusion.

End
- State conclusion.
- State action reader should take.

Apply colors that follow the theme you have chosen for company documents. Save the document.

Part
3

Nickell Industries does business in other countries, including Mexico. One of the executives in the Finance Department has asked you to translate into Spanish some terms that will be used to develop an invoice. Create a document that translates the following terms from English to Spanish and also include in the document the steps for translating text. Your reason for doing this is that if the executives know the steps, they can translate the text at their own computers.

- city
- telephone
- invoice
- product
- description
- total

Format the document with the theme you have chosen for company documents and add any other enhancements to improve the appearance of the document. Save the completed document and name it **2-NITranslations**. Print and then close **2-NITranslations**.

Part

4

While working on the writing manual for Nickell Industries, you decide to purchase some reference books on grammar and punctuation. Using the internet, search for books that provide information on grammar and punctuation and then choose three books. You know that the books will be purchased soon, so you decide to add the information in the writing manual document, telling readers what reference books are available. Include this information on a separate page at the end of the text in **2-NIManual**. Save, print, and then close the document.

Inserting Headers, Footers, and References

 The online course includes additional review and assessment resources.

Skills Assessment

Assessment 1

Insert Specialized Footers in a Report

1. Open **Robots** and then save it with the name **3-Robots**.
2. Keep the heading *NAVIGATION* together with the paragraph of text that follows it.
3. Move the insertion point to the beginning of the document and then create an odd page footer that includes the following:
   a. Insert the current date at the left margin. (Choose the date option that displays the month spelled out, such as *January 1, 2021*.)
   b. Using the Pictures button in the Insert group on the Header & Footer Tools Design tab, insert the **Robot** image file in the middle of the footer. Change the height of the robot image to 0.5 inch and the text wrapping to Behind Text. Drag the robot image below the footer pane border.
   c. At the right margin, type Page, press the spacebar, and then insert a plain page number at the current position.
4. Create an even page footer that includes the following:
   a. At the left margin, type Page, press the spacebar, and then insert a plain page number at the current position.
   b. Insert the **Robot** image file in the middle of the footer and apply the same formatting as you did to the image in the odd page footer.
   c. Insert the current date at the right margin in the same format you chose for the odd page footer.
5. Save, print, and then close **3-Robots**.

Assessment 2

Insert a Header and Footer in a Report on All Pages Except the First Page

1. Open **Volcanoes** and then save it with the name **3-Volcanoes**.
2. Create a header for all pages except the first page and type Volcano Report at the right margin of the Header pane. (Make sure the First Page Header pane is blank.)
3. Create a footer for all pages except the first page and insert the Banded predesigned footer in the Footer pane. (Make sure the First Page Footer pane is blank.)
4. Save, print, and then close **3-Volcanoes**.

Assessment 3

Insert a Section Break and Format and Print Sections

1. Open **CompViruses** and then save it with the name **3-CompViruses**.
2. Insert a section break that begins a new page at the beginning of the title *CHAPTER 2 SECURITY RISKS*.
3. Move the insertion point to the beginning of the document and then create a footer for the first section in the document with *Chapter 1* at the left margin, the page number in the middle, and your first and last names at the right margin.
4. Edit the footer for the second section to Chapter 2 instead of Chapter 1. *Hint: Make sure you break the link*.
5. Print only the pages in section 2.
6. Save and then close **3-CompViruses**.

Assessment 4

Insert Footnotes in a Newsletter

1. Open **DesignNwsltr** and then save it with the name **3-DesignNwsltr**.
2. Create the first footnote shown in Figure 3.1 at the end of the first paragraph in the *Applying Guidelines* section.
3. Create the second footnote shown in the figure at the end of the last paragraph in the *Applying Guidelines* section.
4. Create the third footnote shown in the figure at the end of the only paragraph in the *Choosing Paper Size and Type* section.
5. Create the fourth footnote shown in the figure at the end of the only paragraph in the *Choosing Paper Weight* section.
6. Save and then print **3-DesignNwsltr**.
7. Select the entire document and then change the font to Constantia.
8. Select all the footnotes and then change the font to Constantia. *Note: Pressing Ctrl + A will select all the footnotes in the document*.
9. Delete the second footnote (*Maddock*).
10. Save, print, and then close **3-DesignNwsltr**.

Figure 3.1 Assessment 4

James Haberman, "Designing a Newsletter," *Desktop Designs* (2021): 23-29.

Arlita Maddock, "Guidelines for a Better Newsletter," *Desktop Publisher* (2020): 32-38.

Monica Alverso, "Paper Styles for Newsletters," *Design Technologies* (2021): 45-51.

Keith Sutton, "Choosing Paper Styles," *Design Techniques* (2021): 8-11.

Assessment 5

Insert Sources and Citations in a Privacy Rights Document

1. Open **PrivRights** and then save it with the name **3-PrivRights**.
2. Make sure that MLA style is selected in the Citations & Bibliography group on the References tab.
3. With the insertion point positioned at the beginning of the document, type your name, press the Enter key, type your instructor's name, press the Enter key, type the title of your course, press the Enter key, type the current date, and then press the Enter key. Type the title Privacy Rights and then center the title.
4. The text in the document is set in 12-point Cambria. Make this the default font for the document. *Hint: Do this with the Set As Default button at the Font dialog box*.

5. Insert a header that displays your last name and the page number at the right margin.
6. Select and then delete the text *(Hartley)* that appears in the second paragraph.
7. With the insertion point positioned between the word *policy* and the period that ends the third sentence in the second paragraph, press the spacebar and then insert the source information for a journal article written by Kenneth Hartley using the following information:

Author	Kenneth Hartley
Title	Privacy Laws
Journal Name	Business World
Year	2021
Pages	24-46
Volume	XII

8. Select and then delete the text *(Ferraro)* that appears in the second paragraph.
9. With the insertion point positioned between the word *place* and the period that ends the fourth sentence in the second paragraph, press the spacebar and then insert the following source information for a book:

Author	Ramona Ferraro
Title	Business Employee Rights
Year	2021
City	Tallahassee
Publisher	Everglades Publishing House

10. Select and then delete the text *(Aldrich)* that appears in the last paragraph.
11. With the insertion point positioned between the word *limit"* and the period that ends the second sentence in the last paragraph, press the spacebar and then insert the following information for an article in a periodical:

Author	Kelly Aldrich
Title	What Rights Do Employees Have?
Periodical Title	Great Plains Times
Year	2021
Month	May
Day	6
Pages	18-22

12. Insert page number 20 in the Kelly Aldrich citation using the Edit Citation dialog box.
13. Edit the Kenneth Hartley source title to read *Small Business Privacy Laws* in the *Master List* section of the Source Manager dialog box. (Update both the Master List and the Current List.)
14. Select and delete the last two sentences in the second paragraph and then delete the Ramona Ferraro source in the *Current List* section of the Source Manager dialog box.
15. Insert a works cited page on a separate page at the end of the document.
16. Create a new source in the document using the Source Manager dialog box and include the following source information for a website:

Author	Harold Davidson
Name of Web Page	Small Business Policies and Procedures
Year	2020
Month	December
Day	12
Year Accessed	2021
Month Accessed	February
Day Accessed	23
URL	https://ppi-edu.net/policies

17. Insert a citation for Harold Davidson at the end of the last sentence in the first paragraph.
18. Update the works cited page.
19. Format the works cited page to meet MLA requirements with the following changes:
    a. Select the *Works Cited* heading and all the entries and then click the *No Spacing* style.
    b. Change the spacing to 2.0.
    c. Format the works cited entries with a hanging indent.
    d. Center the title *Works Cited*.
20. Save and then print **3-PrivRights**.
21. Change the document and works cited page from MLA style to APA style. Make sure you change the title of the sources list to *References*. Select the references in the list and then change the line spacing to double spacing.
22. Save the document **3-PrivRights**, print page 2, and then close **3-PrivRights**.

Visual Benchmark

Format a Report in MLA Style

1. Open **SecurityDefenses** and then save it with the name **3-SecurityDefenses**.
2. Format the document so it displays as shown in Figure 3.2 with the following specifications:
   a. Change the document font to 12-point Cambria and then set 12-point Cambria as the default.
   b. Use the information from the works cited page when inserting citations into the document. The Hollingsworth citation is for a journal article, the Montoya citation is for a book, and the Gillespie citation is for a website.
   c. Format the works cited page to meet MLA requirements.
3. Save, print, and then close **3-SecurityDefenses**.

Figure 3.2 Visual Benchmark

Last Name 3

Works Cited

Gillespie, Julietta. *Creating Computer Security Systems.* 21 August 2021. 8 September 2021.

<https://ppi-edu.net/publishing>.

Hollingsworth, Melanie. "Securing Vital Company Data." *Corporate Data Management*

(2021): 8-11.

Montoya, Paul. *Designing and Building Secure Systems.* San Francisco: Golden Gate, 2020.

Page 3

Last Name 2

More and more people are using software products that deal with both viruses and spyware in one package. Some can be set to protect your computer in real time, meaning that they detect an incoming threat, alert you, and stop it before it is downloaded to your computer. In addition to using antivirus and antispyware software, consider allowing regular updates to your operating system. Companies release periodic updates that address flaws in their shipped software or new threats that have come on the scene since their software shipped (Hollingsworth).

Page 2

Last Name 1

Student Name

Instructor Name

Course Title

Current Date

Security Defenses

Whether protecting a large business or your personal laptop, certain security defenses are available that help prevent attacks and avoid data loss, including firewalls and software that detects and removes malware.

A firewall is a part of your computer system that blocks unauthorized access to your computer or network even as it allows authorized access. You can create firewalls using software, hardware, or a combination of software and hardware (Hollingsworth). Firewalls are like guards at the gate of the Internet. Messages that come into or leave a computer or network go through the firewall, where they are inspected. Any message that does not meet preset criteria for security is blocked. "You can set up trust levels that allow some types of communications through and block others, or designate specific sources of communications that should be allowed access" (Montoya 15).

All computer users should consider using antivirus and antispyware software to protect their computers, data, and privacy. Antivirus products require that you update the virus definitions on a regular basis to ensure that you have protection from new viruses as they are introduced. Once you have updated definitions, you run a scan and have several options: to quarantine viruses to keep your system safe from them, to delete a virus completely, and to report viruses to the antivirus manufacturer to help keep their definitions current. Antispyware performs a similar function regarding spyware (Gillespie).

Page 1

Case Study

Part 1

You just opened a new company, Chrysalis Media, that helps businesses creatively communicate with customers. Some of the media design services you offer are business letterhead, logos, flyers, newsletters, signage, and business cards. Create a company letterhead document by opening a blank document and then inserting the **CMHdr** image file as a first page header. Change the height of the image to 1.4" and change the header position from the top to 0.3". Insert the **CMFtr** image file as a first page footer. Save the completed letterhead document and name it **3-CMLtrhd**. Print and then close the document.

Part 2

You have a document on defining newsletter elements that you want to make available to clients. Open **Nwsltr-Define** and then save it with the name **3-Nwsltr-Define**. Create a header for all the pages except the first page and insert the **CMHdr** image file in the Header pane. Change the width of the image to 2" and change the header position from the top to 0.3". Insert a footer with the page number at the bottom center of each page. Save, print, and then close **3-Nwsltr-Define**.

Part 3

You want to provide information for employees on designing newsletters and have a report on newsletter design that needs to be formatted into the APA style. Open **CM-DesignNwsltr** and then save it with the name **3-CM-DesignNwsltr-APA**. Look at the information in Figure 3.1 (on page 14) and then insert the information as in-text journal article citations in the locations indicated in Steps 2 through 5 in Assessment 4. However, position the insertion point inside the period before inserting the citation. Add a reference page on a separate page at the end of the document. Center the title *References* and change the title to all uppercase letters. Select the entire document and change the font to 12-point Cambria. Apply any other formatting to follow APA guidelines. Save **3-CM-DesignNwsltr-APA**.

Part 4

You want to include some additional information on newsletter guidelines. Using the internet, look for websites that provide information on desktop publishing and/or newsletter design. Include in the **3-CM-DesignNwsltr-APA** report document at least one additional paragraph with information you found on the internet and include a citation for each source from which you have borrowed information. Save, print, and then close the report.

The online course includes additional review and assessment resources.

Skills Assessment

Assessment

1

Create and Update a Table of Contents for a Photography Report

1. Open **PhotoRpt** and then save it with the name **4-PhotoRpt**.
2. Move the insertion point to the beginning of the heading *Photography* and then insert a section break that begins a new page.
3. With the insertion point positioned below the section break, insert a page number at the bottom center of each page and change the beginning number to *1*.
4. Press Ctrl + Home to move the insertion point to the beginning of the document (on the blank page) and then create a table of contents with the *Automatic Table 1* option at the Table of Contents button drop-down list.
5. Display the Table of Contents dialog box, change the *Formats* option to *Distinctive*, and make sure a *3* displays in the *Show levels* measurement box.
6. Change the page number format of the table of contents page to lowercase roman numerals.
7. Save the document and then print only the table of contents page.
8. Insert a page break at the beginning of the heading *Camera Basics*.
9. Update the table of contents.
10. Save the document and then print only the table of contents page.
11. Close **4-PhotoRpt**.

Assessment

2

Insert Captions and a Table of Figures in a Report

1. Open **InputDevices** and then save it with the name **4-InputDevices**.
2. Insert a caption for each of the three images in the document that uses *Figure* as the label, uses an arabic number (1, 2, 3) as the figure number, and displays centered below the image. Use *Keyboard* for the first figure caption, *Mouse* for the second, and *Laptop* for the third.
3. Move the insertion point to the beginning of the title COMPUTER INPUT DEVICES and then insert a section break that begins a new page.
4. Press Ctrl + Home, type Table of Figures, press the Enter key, and then insert a table of figures with the Formal format applied.
5. Apply the Heading 1 style to the title *Table of Figures*.
6. Move the insertion point to the title COMPUTER INPUT DEVICES. Insert a page number at the bottom center of each page and change the starting number to *1*.
7. Move the insertion point to the title TABLE OF FIGURES and then change the page numbering style to lowercase roman numerals.
8. Insert a page break at the beginning of the heading MOUSE.
9. Update the table of figures.
10. Save, print, and then close **4-InputDevices**.

Format and Navigate in a Corporate Report

1. Open **DIReport** and then save it with the name **4-DIReport**.
2. Turn on the display of bookmarks.
3. Move the insertion point to the end of the third paragraph (the paragraph that begins *The audit committee selects*) and then insert a bookmark named *Audit*.
4. Move the insertion point to the end of the first paragraph in the section *FEES TO INDEPENDENT AUDITOR*, following the *(Excel worksheet)* text, and then insert a bookmark named *Audit_Fees*.
5. Move the insertion point to the end of the last paragraph and then insert a bookmark named *Compensation*.
6. Navigate in the document using the bookmarks.
7. Move the insertion point to the end of the first paragraph in the section *COMMITTEE RESPONSIBILITIES*, press the spacebar, and then insert a hyperlink to the Audit_Fees bookmark.
8. Select the text *(Excel worksheet)* at the end of the first paragraph in the section *FEES TO INDEPENDENT AUDITOR* and then insert a hyperlink to the Excel file **AuditorFees**.
9. Move the insertion point to the end of the document, click the image, and then insert a hyperlink to the Word document **DIGraphic**. At the Insert Hyperlink dialog box, create a ScreenTip with the text *Click to view a long-term incentives graphic*.
10. Press and hold down the Ctrl key, click the *(Excel worksheet)* hyperlink, and then release the Ctrl key. Print the Excel worksheet that displays by clicking the File tab, clicking the *Print* option, and then clicking the Print button in the Print backstage area.
11. Close the Excel program without saving the file.
12. Press and hold down the Ctrl key, click the image to display the Word document containing the graphic, and then release the Ctrl key. Print and then close the graphic document.
13. Save, print, and then close **4-DIReport**.

Customize a Table of Contents

1. Open **DIInformation** and then save it with the name **4-DIInformation**.
2. By default, an automatic table of contents is created using text with the Heading 1, Heading 2, and Heading 3 styles applied. The **4-DIInformation** document contains text with Heading 4 applied. Display the Table of Contents Options dialog box and determine how to specify that the table of contents should include text with the Heading 4 style applied. Replace the existing table of contents.
3. Save **4-DIInformation** and then print only section 1 (the two pages of the table of contents).
4. Close **4-DIInformation**.

Visual Benchmark

Create a Table of Contents and a Table of Figures

1. Open **Networks** and then save it with the name **4-Networks**.
2. Format the document so it appears as shown in Figure 4.1 with the following specifications:
   a. Insert the captions for the figures as shown (see Page 3 of the figure).

    b. Insert the table of figures as shown (see Page 2 of the figure) using the *From template* format option with period leaders. Apply the Heading 1 style to the *FIGURES* heading.

    c. Insert the table of contents as shown (see Page 1 of the figure) using the *From template* format option with period leaders. Apply the Heading 1 style to the *TABLE OF CONTENTS* heading.

    d. Insert page numbers at the right margins as shown (see Pages 2, 3, and 4 of the figure).

3. Save, print, and then close **4-Networks**.

Figure 4.1 Visual Benchmark

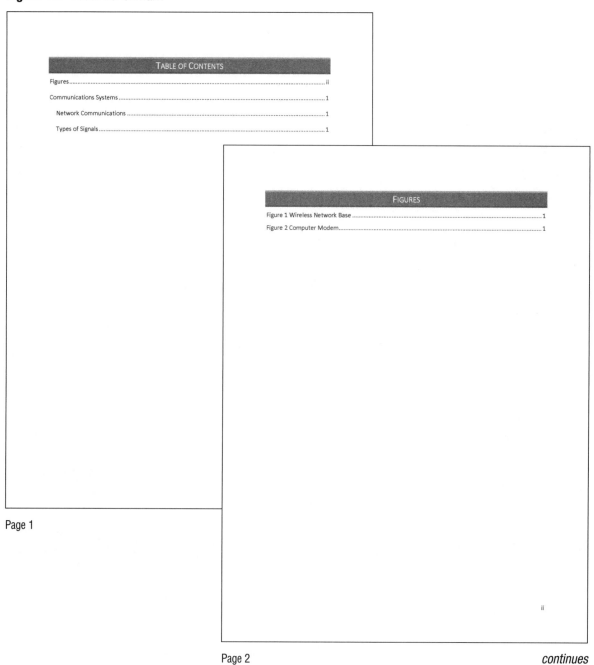

Page 1

Page 2

ii

continues

Figure 4.1 Visual Benchmark—*continued*

COMMUNICATIONS SYSTEMS

A computer network is one kind of communications system. This system includes sending and receiving hardware, transmission and relay systems, common sets of standards so all the equipment can "talk" to each other, and communications software.

NETWORK COMMUNICATIONS

You use such a networked communications system whenever you send/receive IM or email messages, pay a bill online, shop at an Internet store, send a document to a shared printer at work or at home, or download a file.

The world of computer network communications systems is made up of:

- Transmission media upon which the data travels to/from its destination.
- A set of standards and network protocols (rules for how data is handled as it travels along a communications channel). Devices use these to send and receive data to and from each other.
- Hardware and software to connect to a communications pathway from the sending and receiving ends.

Figure 1 Wireless Network Base

The first step in understanding a communications system is to learn the basics about transmission signals and transmission speeds when communicating over a network.

TYPES OF SIGNALS

Two types of signals are used to transmit voices and other so
digital. An analog signal is formed by continuous sound wave
voice is transmitted as an analog signal over traditional telep
signal uses a discrete signal that is either high or low. In com
1, and low represents the digital bit 0. These are the only two

Telephone lines carry your voice using an analog signal. How
rather, they use a binary system of
signals. If you send data between c
phone line, the signal has to be tra
(modulated) and back again to digi
computer on the receiving end. The

Figure 2 Computer Modem

data from a transmission source such as your telephone line or cable television connection is a modem. The word modem comes from the combination of the words *modulate* and *demodulate*.

Today, most new communications technologies simply use a digital signal, saving the trouble of converting transmissions. An example of this trend is the demise in 2009 of analog television transmissions as the industry switched to digital signals. Many people were sent scrambling to either buy a newer television set or buy a converter to convert digital transmissions back to analog to work with their older equipment. Newer computer networks, too, use a pure digital signal method of sending and receiving data over a network.

2

Page 3

Page 4

Case Study

Part
1

You work in the Human Resources Department at Brennan Distributors and are responsible for preparing an employee handbook. Open **BDEmpHandbook** and then save it with the name **4-BDEmpHandbook**. Apply the following specifications to the document:

- Insert a page break before each centered title (except the first title, *Introduction*).
- Apply the Heading 1 style to the titles and the Heading 2 style to the headings.
- Apply a style set of your choosing.
- Apply a theme that makes the handbook easy to read.
- Insert a table of contents.
- Insert appropriate page numbering. ***Hint: Insert a* Next Page *section break at the beginning of the title* Introduction**.
- Insert a cover page and insert the appropriate text in the placeholders. Delete any extra placeholders.
- Add any other elements that will improve the appearance of the document.

Save, print, and then close **4-BDEmpHandbook**.

Part
2

Open **NavigateWeb** and then save it with the name **4-NavigateWeb**. Apply the following specifications to the document:

- Position the insertion point in the first table and then use the caption feature to create the caption *Table 1: Common Top-Level Domain Suffixes* above the table.
- Position the insertion point in the second table and then create the caption *Table 2: Common Search Tools*.
- Position the insertion point in the third table and then create the caption *Table 3: Advanced Search Parameters*.
- Insert a table of contents. (Apply the Heading 1 style to the Table of Contents heading.)
- Insert a table of figures on the page following the table of contents. (Apply the Heading 1 style to the Table of Figures heading and then update the table of contents to include a reference to the Table of Figures.)
- Insert appropriate page numbers.
- Check the page breaks in the document. If a heading displays at the bottom of a page and the paragraph of text that follows displays at the top of the next page, format the heading so it stays with the paragraph. ***Hint: Do this at the Paragraph dialog box with the Line and Page Breaks tab selected***.
- If necessary, update the table of contents and the table of figures.

Save, print, and then close **4-NavigateWeb**.

Part
3

Send an email to your instructor detailing the steps you followed to create the table captions. Attach **4-NavigateWeb** to the email.

Microsoft
Word Level 2

Unit 1 Performance Assessment

 Data Files

Before beginning unit work, copy the WL2U1 folder to your storage medium and then make WL2U1 the active folder.

Assessing Proficiency

In this unit, you have learned to apply advanced character formatting; insert symbols and special characters; find and replace formatting, special characters, styles, and using wildcard characters; manage, inspect, and proof documents; and insert custom headers, footers, and references. You have also learned to create a table of contents and a table of figures and to navigate in a document with the Navigation pane as well as bookmarks, hyperlinks, and cross-references.

Assessment

1

Apply Character Spacing and OpenType Features

1. Open **CVTakeoutMenu** and then save it with the name **U1-CVTakeoutMenu**.
2. Select the title *Take Out Menu*, change the character spacing to Expanded by 1.5 points, turn on kerning, apply Stylistic Set 5, and use contextual alternates.
3. Select the heading *Soups*, change the font size to 22 points, change the character spacing to Expanded, turn on kerning, and apply Stylistic Set 5.
4. Apply the same formatting applied to the heading *Soups* in Step 3 to the other headings (*Salads*, *Main Dishes*, and *Desserts*).
5. Select the last sentence in the document (the sentence that begins *Enjoy the tastes*) and then turn on kerning and apply Stylistic Set 5.
6. Save, print, and then close **U1-CVTakeoutMenu**.

Assessment

2

Find and Replace Formatting and Use a Wildcard Character

1. Open **Agreement** and then save it with the name **U1-Agreement**.
2. Find text set in the *+Headings* font and replace the font with Corbel.
3. Find text set in the *+Body* font and replace the font with Candara.
4. Using a wildcard character, find all occurrences of *Pin?h?rst?Mad?s?n Builders* and replace them with *Pinehurst-Madison Builders*. (Make sure you remove the formatting option from the *Find what* and *Replace with* text boxes.)

5. Using a wildcard character, find all occurrences of *?erry L?w?ndowsk?* and replace them with *Gerry Lewandowski*.
6. Save, print, and then close **U1-Agreement**.

<table>
<tr><td>Assessment
3</td><td>

Sort Text

1. Open **SHSSort** and then save it with the name **U1-SHSSort**.
2. Select the five clinic names, addresses, and telephone numbers below the heading *SUMMIT HEALTH SERVICES* and then sort the text alphabetically in ascending order by clinic name.
3. Sort the three columns of text below the heading *EXECUTIVE TEAM* by the extension number in ascending order.
4. Sort the text in the table in the *First Half Expenses* column numerically in descending order.
5. Save, print, and then close **U1-SHSSort**.

</td></tr>
</table>

<table>
<tr><td>Assessment
4</td><td>

Insert Document Properties and Inspect a Health Plan Document

1. Open **KLHPlan** and then save it with the name **U1-KLHPlan**.
2. Display the U1-KLHPlan Properties dialog box, type the following in the specified text boxes, and then close the dialog box:

Title	Key Life Health Plan
Subject	Company Health Plan
Author	(Insert your first and last names)
Category	Health Plan
Keywords	health, plan, network
Comments	This document describes highlights of the Key Life Health Plan.

3. Save the document and then print only the document properties.
4. Inspect the document and remove any hidden text.
5. Check the accessibility of the document. Type the alternate text Key Life Logo for the image (a key with *KEY LIFE* on the key) and the alternate text KLHP SmartArt including Compassion, Quality, and Commitment for the SmartArt diagram.
6. Save, print, and then close **U1-KLHPlan**.

</td></tr>
</table>

<table>
<tr><td>Assessment
5</td><td>

Proof and Insert Custom Footers for a Building Website Document

1. Open **BuildWebsite** and then save it with the name **U1-BuildWebsite**.
2. Display the Word Options dialog box with *Proofing* selected in the left panel, remove the check mark in the *Ignore words in UPPERCASE* check box, insert a check mark in the *Show readability statistics* check box, and then close the dialog box.
3. Complete a spelling and grammar check on the document.
4. Create a custom odd page footer that prints the document title, *Building a Website*, at the left margin and the page number at the right margin. Also create a custom even page footer that prints the page number at the left margin and the document title at the right margin.
5. Display the Word Options dialog box with *Proofing* selected in the left panel, insert a check mark in the *Ignore words in UPPERCASE* check box, remove the check mark in the *Show readability statistics* check box, and then close the dialog box.
6. Save, print, and then close **U1-BuildWebsite**.

</td></tr>
</table>

Assessment 6

Insert Footnotes in a Desktop Publishing Report

1. Open **DTP** and then save it with the name **U1-DTP**.
2. Insert the first footnote shown in Figure U1.1 at the end of the second paragraph in the section *Defining Desktop Publishing*.
3. Insert the second footnote shown in the figure at the end of the fourth paragraph in the section *Defining Desktop Publishing*.
4. Insert the third footnote shown in the figure at the end of the second paragraph in the section *Planning the Publication*.
5. Insert the fourth footnote shown in the figure at the end of the last paragraph in the document.
6. Keep the heading *Planning the Publication* together with the paragraph of text that follows it.
7. Save and then print **U1-DTP**.
8. Select the entire document and then change the font to Constantia.
9. Select all the footnotes and then change the font to Constantia.
10. Delete the third footnote.
11. Save, print, and then close **U1-DTP**.

Figure U1.1 Assessment 6

Laurie Fellers, *Desktop Publishing Design* (Dallas: Cornwall & Lewis, 2021), 67-72.

Joel Moriarity, "The Desktop Publishing Approach," *Desktop Publishing* (2021): 3-6.

Jin Loh, *Desktop Publishing with Style* (Los Angeles: Monroe-Ackerman, 2020), 89-93.

Andrew Rushton, *Desktop Publishing Tips and Tricks* (Minneapolis: Aurora, 2021), 103-106.

Assessment 7

Create Citations and Prepare a Works Cited Page for a Report

1. Open **DesignWebsite** and then save it with the name **U1-DesignWebsite**.
2. Format the title page to meet Modern Language Association (MLA) style requirements with the following changes:
   a. Make sure that MLA style is selected in the Citations & Bibliography group on the References tab.
   b. With the insertion point positioned at the beginning of the document, type your name, press the Enter key, type your instructor's name, press the Enter key, type the title of your course, press the Enter key, type the current date, and then press the Enter key. Type the title Designing a Website and then center the title.
   c. The text in the document is set in 12-point Cambria. Make this the default font for the document.
   d. Insert a header that displays your last name and the page number at the right margin.

3. Select and then delete the text *(Mercado)* in the second paragraph of text. With the insertion point positioned between the word *users* and the period that ends the sentence, press the spacebar and then insert the source information from a journal article using the following information:

Author	Claudia Mercado
Title	Connecting a Web Page
Journal Name	Connections
Year	2021
Pages	12-21
Volume	4

4. Select and then delete the text *(Holmes)* in the second paragraph of text. With the insertion point positioned between the word *routing* and the period that ends the sentence, press the spacebar and then insert the source information from a website using the following information:

Author	Brent Holmes
Name of Web Page	Hosting Your Web Page
Year	2020
Month	September
Day	20
Year Accessed	(type current year)
Month Accessed	(type current month)
Day Accessed	(type current day)
URL	https://ppi-edu.net/webhosting

5. Select and then delete the text *(Vukovich)* in the last paragraph of text. With the insertion point positioned between the word *hyperlinks"* and the period that ends the sentence, press the spacebar and then insert the source information from a book using the following information:

Author	Ivan Vukovich
Title	Computer Technology in the Business Environment
Year	2021
City	San Francisco
Publisher	Gold Coast

6. Insert the page number *20* in the citation by Ivan Vukovich using the Edit Citation dialog box.
7. Edit the Ivan Vukovich source by changing the last name to *Vulkovich* in the *Master List* section of the Source Manager dialog box. Click Yes at the message asking about updating the source in both the *Master List* and the *Current List* sections.
8. Create a new source in the document using the Source Manager dialog box and include the following source information for a journal article:

Author	Sonia Jaquez
Title	Organizing a Web Page
Journal Name	Design Techniques
Year	2021
Pages	32-44
Volume	9

9. Type the following sentence at the end of the last paragraph in the document: Browsers look for pages with these names first when a specific file at a website is requested, and index pages display by default if no other page is specified.
10. Insert a citation for Sonia Jaquez at the end of the sentence you just typed.
11. Insert a citation for Claudia Mercado following the second sentence in the first paragraph of the document.

12. Insert a works cited page at the end of the document on a separate page.
13. Format the works cited page as follows to meet MLA requirements:
    a. Select the *Works Cited* title and all the entries and then click the *No Spacing* style.
    b. Change the line spacing to double spacing.
    c. Center the title *Works Cited*.
    d. Format the works cited entries with a hanging indent. ***Hint: Use Ctrl + T to create a hanging indent***.
14. Save and then print **U1-DesignWebsite**.
15. Change the document and works cited page from MLA style to APA style. Change the title *Works Cited* to *References*. Select the references in the list and then change the line spacing to double spacing with 0 points of spacing after paragraphs.
16. Save **U1-DesignWebsite**, print page 3, and then close the document.

Assessment 8

Create Captions and Insert a Table of Figures in a Report

1. Open **SoftwareCareers** and then save it with the name **U1-SoftwareCareers**.
2. Click in the first table and then insert the caption *Table 1 Software Development Careers* above the table. (Change the paragraph spacing after the caption to 3 points.)
3. Click in the second table and then insert the caption *Table 2 Application Development Careers* above the table. (Change the paragraph spacing after the caption to 3 points.)
4. Move the insertion point to the beginning of the heading *SOFTWARE DEVELOPMENT CAREERS* and then insert a section break that begins a new page.
5. With the insertion point below the section break, insert a page number at the bottom center of each page and change the starting page number to *1*.
6. Move the insertion point to the beginning of the document and then insert the *Automatic Table 1* table of contents.
7. Press Ctrl + Enter to insert a page break.
8. Type Tables, press the Enter key, and then insert a table of figures using the Formal format.
9. Apply the Heading 1 style to the title *Tables*.
10. Move the insertion point to the beginning of the document and then change the number format to lowercase roman numerals.
11. Update the entire table of contents.
12. Save, print, and then close **U1-SoftwareCareers**.

Writing Activities

Activity 1

Prepare an APA Guidelines Document

You work for a psychiatric medical facility and many of the psychiatrists and psychiatric nurses you work with submit papers to journals that require formatting in APA style. Your supervisor has asked you to prepare a document that describes the APA guidelines and provides the steps for formatting a Word document in APA style. Find a website that provides information on APA style and include the hyperlink in your document. (Consider websites for writing labs at colleges and universities.) Apply formatting to enhance the appearance of the document. Save the document and name it **U1-APA**. Print and then close **U1-APA**.

Activity

2

Create a Rental Form Template

You work in a real estate management company that manages rental houses. You decide to automate the standard rental form that is normally filled in by hand. Open **LeaseAgreement** and then save the document and name it **U1-LeaseAgreement**. Look at the lease agreement document and determine how to automate it so it can be filled in using the Find and Replace feature in Word. Change the current *Lessor* and *Lessee* names to *LESSOR* and *LESSEE*. Save the document as a template named **LeaseForm** in your WL2U1 folder. Use File Explorer to open a document based on the **LeaseForm** template. Find and replace the following text (use your judgment about which occurrences should be changed and which should not):

DAY	22nd
MONTH	February
YEAR	2021
RENT	$950
DEPOSIT	$500
LESSOR	Samantha Herrera
LESSEE	Daniel Miller

Save the document and name it **U1-Lease1**. Print and then close **U1-Lease1**. Use File Explorer to open a document based on the **LeaseForm** template and then create another rental document. You determine the text to replace with the standard text. Save the completed rental document and name it **U1-Lease2**. Print and then close **U1-Lease2**.

Internet Research

Create a Job Search Report

Use a search engine to locate companies that offer jobs in a field in which you are interested in working. Locate at least three websites that identify employment opportunities and then create a report in Word that includes the following information about each site:

- Name and URL
- A brief description
- Employment opportunities available

Create a hyperlink from your report to each site and include any additional information pertinent to the site. Apply formatting to enhance the document. Save the document and name it **U1-JobSearch**. Print and then close **U1-JobSearch**.

Microsoft®

Word Level 2

Unit 2

Editing and Formatting Documents

Customizing Objects and Creating Charts

 The online course includes additional review and assessment resources.

Skills Assessment

Assessment
1

Insert and Customize an Image and Text Box in a Timeline Document

1. Open **Timeline** and then save it with the name **5-Timeline**.
2. Move the insertion point to the right of the text *Electronic Commerce* (item 2).
3. Display the Insert Picture dialog box, navigate to your WL2C5 folder, and then double-click the ***CreditCard*** image file.
4. Customize the image so it appears as shown in Figure 5.1 by completing the following steps:
   a. Change the height of the image to 1.8 inches.
   b. Change the text wrapping to Square.
   c. Display the Layout dialog box with the Position tab selected.
   d. Precisely position the image on the page with an absolute horizontal measurement of 4.5 inches to the right of the left margin and an absolute vertical measurement of 5.3 inches below the page.
   e. Display the Format Picture task pane with the Effects icon active.
   f. Click *Shadow* to expand the shadow options.
   g. Apply the Offset: Top Left shadow effect (last option in the *Outer* section).
   h. Change the shadow color to Dark Blue (ninth option in the *Standard Colors* section). (Do this with the Color button in the *Shadow* section of the Format Picture task pane.)
   i. Click *Artistic Effects* to expand the options and then apply the Paint Strokes artistic effect (second column, second row in the drop-down gallery). (Do this with the Artistic Effects button in the *Artistic Effects* section of the task pane.)
   j. Close the Format Picture task pane.
5. Move the insertion point to the end of the document and then insert the text *Cell phones* and *Apple Pay* in text boxes as shown in Figure 5.2 with the following specifications:
   a. Insert a text box below the arrow line on page 2 and then type Cell phones in the text box.
   b. Use the Text Direction button to rotate the text in the text box 270 degrees.
   c. Remove the outline from the text box. (Do this with the Shape Outline button in the Shape Styles group.)
   d. Change the text wrapping to Behind Text.
   e. Drag the text box so it is positioned as shown in Figure 5.2.
   f. Complete similar steps to create the text box with the text *Apple Pay* and position the text box as shown in the figure.
6. Save, print, and then close **5-Timeline**.

Figure 5.1 Assessment 1, Step 4

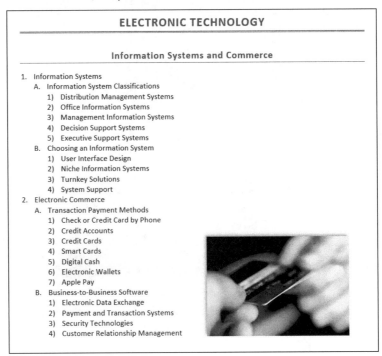

Figure 5.2 Assessment 1, Step 5

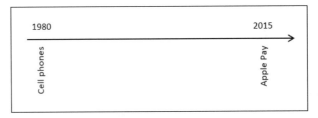

Format a Shape and Edit Points and Wrap Points

1. Open **CedarMeadows** and then save it with the name **5-CedarMeadows**.
2. Select the shape in the document, display the Format Shape task pane (click the Shape Styles group task pane launcher on the Drawing Tools Format tab), and then apply the following formatting:
   a. Apply the Bottom Spotlight - Accent 5 gradient fill (fifth column, fourth row).
   b. Apply the Inside: Bottom shadow effect (second column, third row in the *Inner* section).
   c. Close the Format Shape task pane.
3. Display editing points around the shape and then adjust the points so they display in a manner similar to what is shown in Figure 5.3. (Click outside the shape after adjusting the editing points.)
4. Select the shape, display the wrap points, and then adjust the wrap points so they display in a manner similar to what is shown in Figure 5.3. (Click outside the shape after adjusting the wrap points.)
5. Save, print, and then close **5-CedarMeadows**.

Figure 5.3 Assessment 2

Cedar Meadows

A typical day at Cedar Meadows begins with a ride up the Alpine Express. At the top, the air is crisp and cool, and the view is unlike anything you have ever seen: the deep, dark blue of the sky provides a stark contrast to the line of white at the horizon, where snow divides the lake and the sky.

You push off and begin your descent, trailing a wake of powder. The snow beneath your skis is so dry it squeaks. You do not really care where you are going or how you get there. The important thing is that you are here. Cedar Meadows is a destination where pleasures abound. Here you can feed your spirit with endless excitement and relaxation.

Fast Facts

Cedar Meadows
1-888-555-9885

Terrain: The Cedar Meadows terrain includes 20 percent beginner slopes, 45 percent intermediate slopes, and 35 percent advanced slopes.

Lifts: Cedar Meadows resort has one aerial tram, three high-speed quads, eight triple chairs, seven double chairs, and six surface lifts.

Elevations: The base elevation is 6,540 feet; the summit, 10,040 feet; the vertical drop, 3,500 feet; and the longest run is 5.5 miles.

Ski School: With over 225 certified ski instructors, the Cedar Meadows Ski School offers a variety of programs.

Children's Services: Children ages 4 through 12 can take advantage of the Snow Explorers program, which offers young skiers an exciting adventure in Alpine skiing and snowboarding.

Ski Shuttles: Free ski shuttles travel to the Cedar Meadows resort seven days a week.

Assessment 3

Link Text Boxes

1. Open **ProtectIssues** and then save it with the name **5-ProtectIssues**.
2. Select the text box at the left and link it to the text box at the right.
3. With the insertion point positioned in the text box at the left, insert the file named **ProIssues**. *Hint: Click the Insert tab, click the Object button arrow, and then click the* Text from File *option*.
4. Adjust the columns so all the text fits in the two columns by changing the height of both text boxes to 8.4 inches and the width of both to 3.1 inches.
5. Save, print, and then close **5-ProtectIssues**.

Assessment 4

Customize a 3D Model

1. Open **Announcement** and then save it with the name **5-Announcement**.
2. Select the 3D model (a red square with a cross) and then apply the following formatting:
   a. Apply the Above Front Right 3D model view. (You will need to click the More 3D Model Views button in the 3D Model Views group to display additional views. The Above Front Right view is in the fifth column, second row.)
   b. Change the height of the model to 2.7 inches.
   c. Apply Tight text wrapping.

      d. Precisely position the model on the page with an absolute horizontal measurement of 4.7 inches to the right of the left margin and an absolute vertical measurement of 4.8 inches below the page.

      e. Display the Format 3D Model task pane and then apply the Perspective: Upper Right shadow effect. (To do this, click the Effects icon, click *Shadow* to expand the options, click the Presets button in the *Shadow* section, and then click the *Perspective: Upper Right* option, in the second column, first row in the *Perspective* section.)

3. Select the icon in the upper left corner of the document (a cross in a circle) and then apply the following formatting:

      a. Change the height of the icon to 1.7 inches.

      b. Apply the Light 1 Fill, Colored Outline - Accent 4 graphic style (fifth graphic style in the Graphics Styles gallery).

      c. Change the position of the icon to Position in Top Left with Square Text Wrapping.

      d. Apply the In Front of Text text wrapping.

4. Save, print, and close **5-Announcement**.

Assessment 5

Create and Format a Column Chart and a Pie Chart

1. At a blank document, use the data in Figure 5.4 to create a column chart (using the default chart style at the Insert Chart dialog box) with the following specifications:

      a. Use the Chart Elements button outside the upper right border of the chart to add a data table and remove the legend.

      b. Apply the Style 4 chart style.

      c. Change the chart title to *Units Sold First Quarter*.

      d. Apply the first WordArt style to the chart area.

      e. Change the chart height to 4 inches.

      f. Change the position of the chart to Position in Top Center with Square Text Wrapping.

2. Move the insertion point to the end of the document, press the Enter key two times, and then create a pie chart (using the default pie chart style at the Insert Chart dialog box) with the data shown in Figure 5.5 and with the following specifications:

      a. Apply the Style 3 chart style.

      b. Move the data labels to the inside end of the pie pieces. ***Hint: Click the Chart Elements button that displays outside the upper right corner of the chart, click the arrow at the right of*** Data Labels, ***and then click*** Inside End.

      c. Change the chart title to *Expense Distribution*.

      d. Apply the Colored Outline - Orange, Accent 2 shape style to the title (third shape style).

      e. Change the chart height to 3 inches and the width to 5.5 inches.

      f. Change the position of the chart to Position in Bottom Center with Square Text Wrapping.

3. Save the document and name it **5-ColumnPieCharts**.

4. Print and then close **5-ColumnPieCharts**.

Figure 5.4 Assessment 5, Step 1, Data for Column Chart

Salesperson	January	February	March
Barnett	55	60	42
Carson	20	24	31
Fanning	15	30	13
Han	52	62	58
Mahoney	49	52	39

Figure 5.5 Assessment 5, Step 2, Data for Pie Chart

Category	Percentage
Salaries	67%
Travel	15%
Equipment	11%
Supplies	7%

Assessment

6

Insert a Horizontal Line in a Footer

1. Open a blank document and then insert a horizontal line by clicking the Borders button arrow in the Paragraph group on the Home tab and then clicking *Horizontal Line* at the drop-down list. Click the horizontal line to select it and then right-click the line. Click *Picture* at the shortcut menu and the Format Horizontal Line dialog box displays. Look at the formatting options that are available at the dialog box and then click the Cancel button to close the dialog box. Close the document without saving it.
2. Open **ShopOnline** and then save it with the name **5-ShopOnline**.
3. Keep the heading *ONLINE SHOPPING MALLS* together with the paragraph that follows it.
4. Create a footer that contains a horizontal line in the standard blue color (eighth color option in the *Standard Colors* section) with a height of 3 points.
5. Save, print, and then close **5-ShopOnline**.

Visual Benchmark

Create a Company Chart

1. Open **Blueline** and then save it with the name **5-Blueline**.
2. Select the gears icon and then customize the icon so it appears as shown in Figure 5.6 with the following specifications:
   - Flip the gears icon horizontally.
   - Apply the Colored Fill - Accent 1, Dark 1 Outline graphic style (second column, third row in the Graphics Styles group gallery).
   - Apply text wrapping that moves the icon behind text.
   - Size and move the gears icon so it is positioned as shown in Figure 5.6.
3. Create the column chart shown in Figure 5.6 with the following specifications:
   - Choose the 3-D Clustered Column Chart at the Insert Chart dialog box.
   - Use the information shown in the chart in the figure to create the data for the chart. (You will need to decrease the size of the data range by one column.)
   - Add a data table to the chart.
   - Change the color of the 2021 series to Dark Blue.
   - Make any other changes so your chart appears similar to the chart in the figure.
4. Save, print, and then close **5-Blueline**.

Figure 5.6 Visual Benchmark

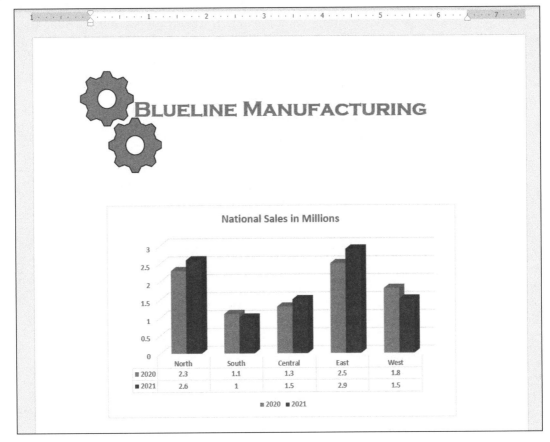

Case Study

Part 1

You are the office manager for Hometown Music, a music store in your town. You have been asked by the owner to create a new letterhead for the music store. Open a blank document, create a custom first page header, and then create a letterhead for the store in the First Page Header pane. Use an image in the letterhead. Some possible images are available in your WL2C5 folder and begin with *Music*. Include an address for the music store and use your town, state, and zip code in the letterhead; also include a telephone number. (The address and phone number can be inserted in the First Page Footer pane rather than the First Page Header pane.) In the First Page Footer pane, insert three icons in the footer, including the eye icon (in the *Analytics* category), the heart icon (in the *Signs and Symbols* category), and the music note icon (in the *Arts* category). (These icons represent the saying "I love music.") Customize, size, and position the icons in the First Page Footer pane. Save the completed letterhead document and name it **5-HMLtrhd**. Save **5-HMLtrhd** as a template in your WL2C5 folder and name the template **5-HMLtrhd-Template**. Close **5-HMLtrhd-Template**.

Part 2

The owner of Hometown Music would like to have a chart of the percentage breakdown of income for the year. Open **HMIncome**, print the document, and then close it. Use File Explorer to open a document based on the **HMLtrhd-Template** you created in Part 1. Use the information you printed to create a pie chart. Apply formatting and customize the pie chart so it is attractive and easy to understand. Save the completed document and name it **5-HMPieChart**. Print and then close **5-HMPieChart**.

Part 3

You have created an invitation for an upcoming piano recital at Hometown Music. You inserted a 3D model in the invitation and need to customize it so it has more visual impact. Open **HMPianoRecital** and then save it with the name **5-HMPianoRecital**. Select the grand piano 3D model, rotate the image so that the keyboard is facing to the right, increase the size, apply a text wrapping option, and move the piano image into the lower left corner of the invitation. Save, print, and then close **5-HMPianoRecital**.

Part 4

The owner would like to have a flyer describing Hometown Music's instrument rental program that can be distributed at recitals and at local schools. Open **HMRentals**, look at the information, and then create a flyer that includes some of the information in the document. Include visual interest in the flyer by inserting a photograph, picture, icon, and/or 3D model. Format the flyer so it appears similar to other Hometown Music documents you have created. Save the completed flyer and name it **5-HMRentalFlyer**. Print and then close **5-HMRentalFlyer**.

Merging Documents

 The online course includes additional review and assessment resources.

Skills Assessment

Assessment

1

Create a Data Source File

1. At a blank document, display the New Address List dialog box and then display the Customize Address List dialog box. (To do this, click the Mailings tab, click the Select Recipients button, click the *Type a New List* option, and then click the Customize Columns button.)

2. At the Customize Address List dialog box, delete the following fields—*Company Name*, *Country or Region*, *Work Phone*, and *E-mail Address*—and then add a custom field named *Cell Phone*. (Position the *Cell Phone* field after the *Home Phone* field.)

3. Close the Customize Address List dialog box and then type the following information in the New Address List dialog box as the first record:

Title	Mr.
First Name	Tony
Last Name	Benedetti
Address Line 1	1315 Cordova Road
Address Line 2	Apt. 402
City	Santa Fe
State	NM
ZIP Code	87505
Home Phone	(505) 555-0489
Cell Phone	(505) 555-0551

4. Type the following information as the second record:

Title	Ms.
First Name	Theresa
Last Name	Dusek
Address Line 1	12044 Ridgeway Drive
Address Line 2	(leave blank)
City	Santa Fe
State	NM
ZIP Code	87504
Home Phone	(505) 555-1120
Cell Phone	(505) 555-6890

5. Type the following information as the third record:

Title	Ms.
First Name	Mary
Last Name	Arguello
Address Line 1	2554 Country Drive
Address Line 2	#105
City	Santa Fe
State	NM
ZIP Code	87504
Home Phone	(505) 555-7663
Cell Phone	(505) 555-5472

6. Type the following information as the fourth record:

Title	Mr.
First Name	Preston
Last Name	Miller
Address Line 1	120 Second Street
Address Line 2	(leave blank)
City	Santa Fe
State	NM
ZIP Code	87505
Home Phone	(505) 555-3551
Cell Phone	(505) 555-9630

7. Save the data source file and name it **6-CCDS**.
8. Close the blank document without saving changes.

Assessment 2

Create a Letter Main Document and Merge with a Data Source File

1. Open **CCVolunteerLtr** and then save it with the name **6-CCMD**.
2. Select the **6-CCDS** data source file you created in Assessment 1.
3. Move the insertion point to the beginning of the first paragraph of text in the body of the letter, insert the *«AddressBlock»* field, and then press the Enter key two times.
4. Insert the *«GreetingLine»* field specifying a colon rather than a comma as the greeting line format and then press the Enter key two times.
5. Move the insertion point one space to the right of the period that ends the second paragraph of text in the body of the letter and then type the following text inserting the *«Title»*, *«Last_Name»*, *«Home_Phone»*, and *«Cell_Phone»* fields where indicated:

   Currently, *«Title»* *«Last_Name»*, our records indicate your home telephone number is *«Home_Phone»* and your cell phone number is *«Cell_Phone»*. If this information is not accurate, please contact our office with the correct numbers.

6. Merge the main document with all the records in the data source file.
7. Save the merged letters document as **6-CCLetters**.
8. Print and then close **6-CCLetters**.
9. Save and then close **6-CCMD**.

Assessment 3

Create an Envelope Main Document and Merge with a Data Source File

1. Create an envelope main document using the Size 10 envelope size.
2. Select **6-CCDS** as the data source file.
3. Insert the *«AddressBlock»* field in the appropriate location in the envelope document.
4. Merge the envelope main document with all the records in the data source file.
5. Save the merged envelopes document and name it **6-CCEnvs**.
6. Print and then close the envelopes document. (Check with your instructor before printing the envelopes.)
7. Save the envelope main document with the name **6-CCEnvsMD** and then close the document.

Assessment 4

Create a Label Main Document and Merge with a Data Source File

1. Create a label main document using the option *Avery US Letter 5160 Address Labels*.
2. Select **6-CCDS** as the data source file.
3. Insert the *«AddressBlock»* field.
4. Update the labels.
5. Merge the label main document with all the records in the data source file.
6. Select the entire document and then apply the No Spacing style.
7. Save the merged labels document and name it **6-CCLabels**.
8. Print and then close the labels document.
9. Save the label main document with the name **6-CCLabelsMD** and then close the document.

Assessment 5

Edit a Data Source File

1. Open **6-CCMD**. (At the message asking if you want to continue, click Yes.) Save the main document with the name **6-CCMD-A5**.
2. Edit the **6-CCDS** data source file by making the following changes:
   a. Change the address for Ms. Theresa Dusek from *12044 Ridgeway Drive* to *1390 Fourth Avenue*.
   b. Delete the record for Ms. Mary Arguello.
   c. Insert a new record with the following information:
      Mr. Cesar Rivera
      3201 East Third Street
      Santa Fe, NM 87505
      Home Phone: (505) 555-6675
      Cell Phone: (505) 555-3528
3. Merge the main document with all the records in the data source file.
4. Save the merged letters document as **6-CCLtrsEdited**.
5. Print and then close **6-CCLtrsEdited**.
6. Save and then close **6-CCMD-A5**.

Visual Benchmark

Prepare and Merge Letters

1. Open **FPLtrhd** and then save it with the name **6-FPMD**.
2. Look at the information in Figure 6.1 and Figure 6.2 and then use Mail Merge to prepare four letters. (When creating the main document, as shown in Figure 6.2, insert the appropriate fields where you see the text *Title*; *First Name*; *Last Name*; *Street Address*; and *City, State ZIP*. Insert the appropriate fields where you see the text *Title* and *Last Name* in the first paragraph of text.) Create the data source file with customized field names using the information in Figure 6.1 and then save the file and name it **6-FPDS**.
3. Merge the **6-FPMD** main document with the **6-FPDS** data source file and then save the merged letters document and name it **6-FPLtrs**.
4. Print and then close **6-FPLtrs**.
5. Save and then close **6-FPMD**.

Figure 6.1 Visual Benchmark Data Source Records

Mr. Chris Gallagher
17034 234th Avenue
Newport, VT 05855

Ms. Heather Segarra
4103 Thompson Drive
Newport, VT 05855

Mr. Gene Goodrich
831 Cromwell Lane
Newport, VT 05855

Ms. Sonya Kraus
15933 Ninth Street
Newport, VT 05855

Figure 6.2 Visual Benchmark Main Document

FRONTLINE
PHOTOGRAPHY

Current Date

Title First Name Last Name
Street Address
City, State ZIP

Dear Title Last Name:

We have enjoyed being a part of the Newport business community for the past two years. Our success has been thanks to you, Title Last Name, and all our other loyal customers. Thank you for shopping at our store for all of your photography equipment and supply needs.

To show our appreciation for your business, we are enclosing a coupon for 20 percent off any item in our store, including our incredibly low-priced clearance items. Through the end of the month, all camera accessories are on sale. Use your coupon and take advantage of additional savings on items such as camera lenses, tripods, cleaning supplies, and camera bags.

To accommodate our customers' schedules, we have extended our weekend hours. Our store will be open Saturdays until 7:00 p.m. and Sundays, until 5:00 p.m. Come by and let our sales associates find the right camera and accessories for you.

Sincerely,

Student Name

XX
6-FPMD

Enclosure

559 Tenth Street, Suite A, Newport, VT 05855
802.555.4411 ◉ https://ppi-edu.net/frontline

Case Study

Part
1

You are the office manager for Freestyle Extreme, a sporting goods store that specializes in snowboarding and snow skiing equipment and supplies. The store has two branches: one on the east side of town and the other on the west side. One of your job responsibilities is to send letters to customers letting them know about sales, new equipment, and upcoming events. Next month, both stores are having a sale and all snowboarding and snow skiing supplies will be 15 percent off the last marked price.

Create a data source file that contains the following customer information: first name, last name, address, city, state, zip code, and branch. Add six customers to the data source file. Indicate that three usually shop at the East branch and three usually shop at the West branch.

Create a letter as a main document that includes information about the upcoming sale. The letter should contain at least two paragraphs and in addition to the information on the sale, it might include information about the store, snowboarding, and/or snow skiing.

Save the data source file with the name **6-FEDS**, save the main document with the name **6-FEMD**, and save the merged document with the name **6-FELtrs**. Create envelopes for the six merged letters and name the merged envelope document **6-FEEnvs**. Save the envelope main document with the name **6-FEEnvsMD**. Print the merged letters document and the merged envelopes document.

Part
2

A well-known extreme snowboarder will be visiting both branches of Freestyle Extreme to meet with customers and sign autographs. Use the Help feature to learn how to insert an *If...Then...Else...* merge field in a document and then create a letter that includes the name of the extreme snowboarder (you determine the name), the times of the visits to the two branches (1:00 p.m. to 4:30 p.m.), and any additional information that might interest customers. Also include in the letter an *If...Then...Else...* merge field that will insert *Wednesday, September 22* if the customer's branch is *East* and *Thursday, September 23* if the customer's branch is *West*. Add visual interest to the letter by inserting an image, WordArt, or other feature that will attract readers' attention. Save the letter main document and name it **6-SnowMD**. Merge the letter main document with the **6-FEDS** data source file. Save the merged letters document and name it **6-SnowLtrs**. Print the merged letters document.

Part
3

The owner of Freestyle Extreme wants to try selling short skis known as "snow blades" or "skiboards." He has asked you to research these skis and identify one type and model to sell only at the West branch of the store. If the model sells well, the owner will consider selling it at the East branch at a future time. Prepare a main document letter that describes the new snow blade or skiboard that the West branch is going to sell. Include information about pricing and tell customers that they can save 40 percent if they purchase the new item within the next week. Merge the letter main document with the **6-FEDS** data source file and include only those customers that shop at the West branch. Save the merged letters document and name it **6-SBLtrs**. Print the merged letters document. Save the letter main document and name it **6-SBMD**. Save and then close the main document.

Managing Building Blocks and Fields

 The online course includes additional review and assessment resources.

Skills Assessment

Assessment

1

Create Building Blocks

1. Press Ctrl + N to open a blank document and then save the blank document as a template in your WL2C7 folder and name it **7-WLTemplate**. (Make sure you change the *Save as type* option at the Save As dialog box to *Word Template*.)
2. Close **7-WLTemplate**.
3. Use File Explorer to open a document based on **7-WLTemplate** in your WL2C7 folder.
4. Insert **WLFooter** into the document. *Hint: Use the Object button arrow on the Insert tab*.
5. Select the line of text containing the address and telephone number (including the paragraph mark that ends the line). Save the selected text in a custom building block in the Footer gallery; name the building block *WLFooter* and save it in **7-WLTemplate**. *Hint: Use the Footer button to save the content to the Footer gallery*.
6. Select the entire document, press the Delete key, and then insert **WLHeading** into the current document. *Hint: Use the Object button arrow on the Insert tab*.
7. Select the two lines of text (including the paragraph mark at the end of the second line). Save the selected text in a custom building block in the Quick Part gallery; name the building block *WLHeading* and save it in **7-WLTemplate**.
8. Select the entire document and press the Delete key, and then type the text shown in Figure 7.1. (Make sure you apply bold formatting to *Fees:*. If autocorrect superscripts the *th* in *1/6th*, undo the correction.)
9. Select the entire document, save the selected text in a custom building block in the AutoText gallery and name the building block *WLFeesPara* and save it in **7-WLTemplate**.
10. Close the document without saving it. At the message asking if you want to save changes to the template, click the Save button.

Figure 7.1 Assessment 1

Fees: My hourly rate is $350, billed in one-sixth (1/6th) of an hour increments. All time spent on work performed, including meetings, telephone calls, correspondences, and emails, will be billed at the hourly rate set forth in this paragraph. Additional expenses, such as out-of-pocket expenses for postage, courier fees, photocopying charges, and search fees, will be charged at the hourly rate set forth in this paragraph.

Assessment 2

Use Building Blocks to Prepare an Agreement

1. Use File Explorer to open a blank document based on **7-WLTemplate** in your WL2C7 folder.
2. At the blank document, create an agreement with the following specifications:
   a. Insert the *WLHeading* custom building block in the Quick Part gallery.
   b. Press the Enter key and then insert the *WLFeesPara* custom building block in the AutoText gallery.
   c. Insert **WLRepAgrmnt**. *Hint: Use the Object button arrow on the Insert tab*.
   d. Insert the *WLFooter* custom building block. *Hint: Do this with the Footer button*.
3. Click the Close Header and Footer button and then save the completed agreement and name it **7-WLRepAgrmnt**.
4. Print and then close **7-WLRepAgrmnt**.
5. Use File Explorer to open a document based on **7-WLTemplate**.
6. Click the Insert tab, click the Quick Parts button, and then point to *AutoText*.
7. Press the Print Screen button on your keyboard and then click in the document.
8. At the blank document, click the Paste button.
9. Print the document and then close it without saving it.

Assessment 3

Format a Property Protection Report

1. Open **ProtectIssues** and then save it with the name **7-ProtectIssues**.
2. With the insertion point positioned at the beginning of the document, insert the *Automatic Table 2* table of contents building block.
3. Insert the *Banded* header building block, click the *[DOCUMENT TITLE]* placeholder and then type property protection issues.
4. Insert the *Banded* footer building block and then make the document active.
5. Press Ctrl + End to move the insertion point to the end of the document and then insert a field that will insert the file name (without any formatting).
6. Press Shift + Enter and then insert a field that will insert the current date and time (you choose the format).
7. Save, print, and then close **7-ProtectIssues**.

Assessment 4

Insert an Equation Building Block

1. The Building Blocks Organizer dialog box contains a number of predesigned equations that you can insert in a document. At a blank document, display the Building Blocks Organizer dialog box and then insert one of the predesigned equations.
2. Select the equation and then click the Equation Tools Design tab. Notice the groups of commands available for editing an equation.
3. Type the steps you followed to insert the equation and then type a list of the groups available on the Equation Tools Design tab.
4. Save the document and name it **7-Equation**. Print and then close the document.

Visual Benchmark

Create an Agreement with Building Blocks and AutoCorrect Text

1. Use File Explorer to open a document based on **7-WLTemplate**.
2. Create the document shown in Figure 7.2 with the following specifications:
   a. Insert **WLAgreement** into the open document.
   b. At the AutoCorrect dialog box with the AutoCorrect tab selected, create AutoCorrect entries for the text *Woodland Legal Services* (use *wls*) and *Till-Harris Management* (use *thm*).

c. Press Ctrl + Home and then type the first three paragraphs of text shown in Figure 7.2 using the AutoCorrect entries you created.

d. Insert the *WLHeading* building block at the beginning of the document and insert the *WLFooter* building block as a footer.

e. Justify the six paragraphs of text in the document.

3. Save the completed document and name it **7-THMAgrmnt**.

4. Print and then close **7-THMAgrmnt**.

5. Display the AutoCorrect dialog box, delete the *wls* and *thm* entries, and then close the dialog box.

Figure 7.2 Visual Benchmark

REPRESENTATION AGREEMENT

Carlos Sawyer, Attorney at Law

This agreement is made between Carlos Sawyer of Woodland Legal Services and Till-Harris Management for legal services to be provided by Woodland Legal Services.

Legal Representation: Woodland Legal Services will perform the legal services required by Till-Harris Management, keep Till-Harris Management informed of progress and developments, and respond promptly to Till-Harris Management's inquiries and communications.

Attorney's Fees and Costs: Till-Harris Management will pay Woodland Legal Services for attorney's fees for legal services provided under this agreement at the hourly rate of the individuals providing the services. Under this agreement, Till-Harris Management will pay all costs incurred by Woodland Legal Services for representation of Till-Harris Management. Costs will be advanced by Woodland Legal Services and then billed to Till-Harris Management unless the costs can be met from deposits.

Deposit for Fees: Till-Harris Management will pay to Woodland Legal Services an initial deposit of $5,000, to be received by Woodland Legal Services on or before November 1, 2021. Twenty percent of the deposit is nonrefundable and will be applied against attorney's fees. The refundable portion will be deposited by Woodland Legal Services in an interest-bearing trust account. Till-Harris Management authorizes Woodland Legal Services to withdraw the principal from the trust account to pay attorney's fees in excess of the nonrefundable portion.

Statement and Payments: Woodland Legal Services will send Till-Harris Management monthly statements indicating attorney's fees and costs incurred, amounts applied from deposits, and current balance owed. If no attorney's fees or costs are incurred for a month, the statement may be held and combined with that for the following month. Any balance will be paid in full within 30 days after the statement is mailed.

Effective Date of Agreement: The effective date of this agreement will be the date when it is executed by both parties.

Client: _____ Date: _____

Attorney: _____ Date: _____

7110 FIFTH STREET ◆ SUITE 200 ◆ OMAHA NE 68207 ◆ 402-555-7110

Case Study

Part

1

You have been hired as the office manager for Highland Construction Company. The address of the company is 9025 Palmer Park Boulevard, Colorado Springs, CO 80904 and the telephone number is (719) 555-4575. You are responsible for designing business documents that have a consistent visual style and formatting. You decide that your first task is to create a letterhead document. Press Ctrl + N to open a blank document and then save the document as a template named **7-HCCTemplate** in your WL2C7 folder. Close the template document. Use File Explorer to open a document based on **7-HCCTemplate**. At the blank document based on the template, create a letterhead that includes the company name, address, and telephone number, along with an image and/or any other elements to add visual interest. Select the letterhead text and element(s) and then create a building block in the Quick Part gallery named **HCCLtrhd** that is saved in **7-HCCTemplate**. Create the following additional building blocks for your company. (You decide on the names and save the building blocks in **7-HCCTemplate**.)

- Create a building block footer that contains a border line (in a color matching the colors in the letterhead) and the company slogan:

    Colorado Business Since 1985

- Create the following complimentary close building block:

    Sincerely,

    Your Name
    Office Manager

- Create the following company name and address building block:

    Mr. Eric Rashad
    Roswell Industries
    1020 Wasatch Street
    Colorado Springs, CO 80902

- Create the following company name and address building block:

    Ms. Claudia Sanborn
    S & S Supplies
    537 Constitution Avenue
    Colorado Springs, CO 80911

Select and then delete the contents of the document. Close the document without saving it. At the message asking if you want to save changes to the template, click the Save button.

Part

2

Use File Explorer to open a document based on **7-HCCTemplate**. Apply the No Spacing style and then create a letter to Eric Rashad by inserting the Highland Construction Company letterhead (the *HCCLtrhd* building block). Press the Enter key, type today's date, press the Enter key four times, and then insert the *Eric Rashad* building block. Press the Enter key, type an appropriate salutation (such as *Dear Mr. Rashad:*), insert the file named **HCCLetter**, and then insert your complimentary close building block. Finally, insert the footer building block you created for the company. Check the letter and modify the spacing as needed. Save the letter and name it **7-RashadLtr**. Print and then close the letter. Complete similar steps to create a letter to Claudia Sanborn. Save the completed letter and name it **7-SanbornLtr**. Print and then close the letter.

Part 3

Use File Explorer to open a document based on **7-HCCTemplate**. Insert the Highland Construction Company letterhead building block you created in Part 1, type the title *Company Services*, and then insert a SmartArt graphic of your choosing that contains the following text:

Residential Construction
Commercial Construction
Design Consultation
Site Preparation

Apply a heading style to the *Company Services* title, insert the company footer building block, and then save the document and name it **7-CoServices**. Print and then close the document.

CHAPTER

Managing Shared Documents

8

 The online course includes additional review and assessment resources.

Skills Assessment

Assessment 1

Insert Comments in a Web Report

1. Open **NavigateWeb** and then save it with the name **8-NavigateWeb**.
2. Delete the only comment in the document.
3. Position the insertion point at the end of the first paragraph in the section *IPs and URLs* and then insert a comment and type the following comment text: Please identify what the letters ICANN stand for.
4. Position the insertion point at the end of the third paragraph in the section *IPs and URLs* and then insert a comment and type the following comment text: Insert a caption for the following table and the two other tables in the document.
5. Position the insertion point at the end of the last paragraph in the document (above the last table) and insert a comment and type the following comment text: Include in the following table additional examples of methods for narrowing a search.
6. Save the document and then print only the comments.
7. Close **8-NavigateWeb**.

Assessment 2

Track Changes in a Computer Viruses Report

1. Open **CompChapters** and then save it with the name **8-CompChapters**.
2. Turn on Track Changes and then make the following changes:
   a. Edit the first sentence in the document so it displays as follows: *The computer virus is one of the most familiar forms of risk to computer security.*
   b. Type computer's between *the* and *motherboard* in the last sentence in the first paragraph of the document.
   c. Delete the word *real* in the second sentence in the section *Types of Viruses* and then type significant.
   d. Select and then delete the last sentence in the section *Methods of Virus Operation* (which begins *A well-known example of the logic bomb was the*).
   e. Turn off Track Changes.
3. Display the Word Options dialog box with *General* selected and then change the user name to *Stanley Phillips* and the initials to *SP*. Insert a check mark in the *Always use these values regardless of sign in to Office* check box.

4. Turn on Track Changes and then make the following changes:
   a. Delete the words *or cracker* in the seventh sentence in the section *Types of Viruses*.
   b. Delete the word *garner* in the first sentence in the section *CHAPTER 2: SECURITY RISKS* and then type generate.
   c. Select and then move the section *Employee Theft* after the section *Cracking Software for Copying*.
   d. Turn off Track Changes.
5. Display the Word Options dialog box with *General* selected. Change the user name back to the original name and the initials back to the original initials. Also remove the check mark from the *Always use these values regardless of sign in to Office* check box.
6. Print the document. (The document will print with the markups.)
7. Accept all the changes in the document *except* the change moving the section *Employee Theft* after the section *Cracking Software for Copying*; reject this change.
8. Save, print, and then close **8-CompChapters**.

Assessment
3

Restrict Formatting and Editing of a Writing Report

1. Open **WritingProcess** and then save it with the name **8-WritingProcess**.
2. Display the Restrict Editing task pane and then restrict formatting to the Heading 2 and Heading 3 styles. (At the message asking about removing formatting or styles that are not allowed, click No.)
3. Enforce the protection and include the password *writing*.
4. Click the Available styles hyperlink.
5. Apply the Heading 2 style to the two titles *THE WRITING PROCESS* and *REFERENCES*.
6. Apply the Heading 3 style to the seven remaining headings in the document. (The Heading 3 style may not display until the Heading 2 style is applied to the first title.)
7. Close the Styles task pane and then close the Restrict Editing task pane.
8. Save the document and then print only page 1.
9. Close **8-WritingProcess**.

Assessment
4

Insert Comments in a Software Life Cycle Document

1. Open **CommCycle** and then save it with the name **8-CommCycle**.
2. Display the Restrict Editing task pane, restrict editing to comments only, and then start enforcing the protection. (Do not include a password.)
3. At the end of the first paragraph in the document, type the comment Create a SmartArt graphic that illustrates the software life cycle.
4. At the end of the paragraph in the *Design* section, type the comment Include the problem-solving steps.
5. At the end of the paragraph in the *Testing* section, type the comment Describe a typical beta testing cycle.
6. Print only the comments.
7. Close the Restrict Editing task pane.
8. Save and then close **8-CommCycle**.

Track Changes in a Table

1. Open **SalesTable** and then save it with the name **8-SalesTable**.
2. Display the Advanced Track Changes Options dialog box, look at the options for customizing tracked changes in a table, and then make the following changes:
   a. Change the color for inserted cells to Light Purple.
   b. Change the color for deleted cells to Light Green.
3. Turn on Track Changes and then make the following changes:
   a. Insert a new row at the beginning of the table.
   b. Merge the cells in the new row. (At the message stating that the action will not be marked as a change, click OK.)
   c. Type Clearline Manufacturing in the merged cell.
   d. Delete the *Fanning, Andrew* row.
   e. Insert a new row below *Barnet, Jacqueline* and then type Montano, Neil in the first cell, $530,678 in the second cell, and $550,377 in the third cell.
   f. Turn off Track Changes.
4. Save and then print the document. (The document will print with the markups.)
5. Accept all the changes.
6. Display the Advanced Track Changes Options dialog box and then return the color of the inserted cells to Light Blue and the color of the deleted cells to Pink.
7. Save, print, and then close **8-SalesTable**.

Visual Benchmark

Track Changes in an Employee Performance Document

1. Open **NSSEmpPerf** and then save it with the name **8-NSSEmpPerf**.
2. Turn on Track Changes and then make the changes shown in Figure 8.1. (Make the editing changes before moving the *Employment Records* section after the *Performance Evaluation* section.)
3. Turn off Track Changes and then print only the list of markups. *Hint: Do this by displaying the Print backstage area, clicking the first gallery in the Settings category, and then clicking the **List of Markup** option.*
4. Accept all the changes to the document.
5. Save, print, and then close **8-NSSEmpPerf**.

Figure 8.1 Visual Benchmark

Northland Security Systems
3200 North 22ⁿᵈ Street ✦ Springfield ✦ IL ✦ 62102

EMPLOYEE PERFORMANCE

Work Performance Standards

— and/or behavior

(cap)

~~Some~~ work performance standards are written statements of the results/expected of an employee when his or her job elements are satisfactorily performed under existing working conditions. Each employee in a permanent position must be provided with a current set of work performance standards for his or her position.

Employment Records

Your personnel file is maintained in the human resources department, ~~at the main office of Northland Security Systems.~~ The human resources department maintains a file with copies of the documentation in your specific department. Your file includes personnel action documents, mandatory employment forms, your performance evaluations, and documentation of disciplinary action. Your file may include letters of commendation, training certificates, or other work-related documents that your supervisor has requested to be included in your file.

working

Performance Evaluation

— (full-time equivalent)

If you are serving a six-month/probationary period, your supervisor will evaluate your performance at the end of the second and fifth months. If you are completing a one-year probationary period, your evaluations will be conducted at the end of the third, seventh, and eleventh month. You will receive a copy of each performance report. Once you have attained permanent employee status, your performance will be evaluated annually during the month prior to your pay progression date. Each evaluation will include a discussion between you and your supervisor to review and clarify goals and methods to achieve them. The evaluation will also include a/report of your progress on the job. Evaluations will be made with reference to established work performance standards.

written

1-888-555-2200 ✦ https://ppi-edu.net/nss

Case Study

You work for Premier Associates, a career development company that provides career placement, transition, and outplacement for clients. Some of the company's materials need formatting to reflect the company's brand. Open **PALtrhd** and look at the first page header and first page footer. Notice the colors and images used in the header and footer and then close the document. Open **PAResume** and then save it with the name **8-PAResume**. This document has been reviewed by your supervisor, who made her edits as tracked changes. Accept the editing changes to the document and turn off tracked changes. Look at the one comment in the document, make the change mentioned in the comment and then delete the comment. Format the document so it is attractive and easy to read. Consider using the **PAHead** image as a header and **PAFoot** as a footer. Add any additional information to the header or footer that you think is needed. Save, print, and then close **8-PAResume**.

Your supervisor has given you another document that she has edited and wants you to format. Open **PAResumeStyles** and then save it with the name **8-PAResumeStyles**. Accept or reject the edits made by your supervisor and then turn off tracked changes. (The document contains two edits that should be rejected.) Make the change suggested by her comment. Apply formatting to the document similar to what you applied to **8-PAResume**. Save, print, and then close **8-PAResumeStyles**.

Your company provides a sample chonological resume to clients. Your supervisor wants you to open the sample resume and apply formatting to the resume so it has the look and branding of the other Premier Associates documents. Open **PAChronoResume** and then save it with the name **8-PAChronoResume**. Apply formatting so the document has the look of other Premier Associates documents. Save, print, and then close **8-PAChronoResume**.

Your supervisor has asked you to search for a resume template and then download and print it to make it available for clients. Display the New backstage area and search for resumes. Download a resume that looks interesting to you. Apply formatting to the resume so it has the look of the other Premier Associates documents. Save the resume and name it **8-PAWordResume**. Print and then close **8-PAWordResume**.

Microsoft

Word Level 2

Unit 2 Performance Assessment

Assessing Proficiency

In this unit, you have learned to customize objects, create and format charts,
merge documents, apply and customize building blocks, and insert and update
fields. You have also learned to insert and manage comments, track changes, and
restrict and protect documents.

Assessment
1

Insert and Format Objects

1. Open **HMConcert** and then save it with the name **U2-HMConcert**.
2. The border is a drawn image that is positioned in the First Page Header
   pane. Double-click in the header, select the border image, apply the following
   formatting, and then close the First Page Header pane:
   - Apply the Light Gray, Background 2, Darker 10% shape fill (third column,
     second row in the *Theme Colors* section).
   - Apply the Offset: Center shape shadow effect (second column, second row
     in the *Outer* section).
3. Select the image of the music notes and then apply the following formatting:
   - Change the height of the image to 2.5 inches and the width to 4.5 inches.
   - Precisely position the image on the page with an absolute horizontal
     measurement of 0.46 inch to the right of the left margin and an absolute
     vertical measurement of 0.9 inch below the page.
4. Click in the table cell immediately left of the telephone number
   253.555.4500 (you may want to turn on the display of table gridlines), insert
   the telephone icon  (located in the *Communication* category in the Insert
   Icons window), and then apply the following formatting:
   - Change the height of the image to 0.3 inch.
   - Apply the Light 1 Fill, Colored Outline - Accent 3 graphic style (fourth
     style in the Graphic Styles gallery).

5. Click in the table cell immediately left of the email address, insert the envelope icon ⊠ (located in the *Communication* category), and then apply the same formatting to the envelope icon that you applied to the telephone icon.
6. Save, print, and then close **U2-HMConcert**.

Assessment 2

Customize a 3D Model

1. Open **OpenHouse** and then save it with the name **U2-OpenHouse**.
2. Insert a 3D model of a person in a spacesuit located in the Space category at the Online 3D Models window. (Insert the 3D model that does not contain a "runner" badge.) *Note: If you do not have access to the internet, open the OpenHouse-3D document from your WL2U2 folder and then save it with the name U2-OpenHouse.*
3. Select the 3D model of the person in a spacesuit and then apply the following formatting:
   - Rotate the image so the person in the spacesuit is looking more toward his or her right.
   - Increase the height of the image to 4.4 inches.
   - Move the image so it is positioned to the right of *25!* (The image can overlap a portion of the *25!*)
4. Save, print, and then close **U2-OpenHouse**.

Assessment 3

Create and Format a Column Chart

1. At a blank document, use the data in Figure U2.1 to create a column chart with the following specifications:
   a. Choose the 3-D Clustered Column chart type.
   b. Apply the Layout 3 quick layout.
   c. Apply the Style 5 chart style.
   d. Change the chart title to *Yearly Sales*.
   e. Insert a data table with legend keys.

Figure U2.1 Assessment 3

Salesperson	First Half	Second Half
Bratton	$235,500	$285,450
Daniels	$300,570	$250,700
Hughes	$170,200	$180,210
Marez	$308,520	$346,400

f. Select the chart area, apply the Subtle Effect - Green, Accent 6 shape style (last column, fourth row in the *Theme Styles* section), and then apply the Offset: Bottom shadow shape effect (second column, first row in the *Outer* section).

g. Select the series *Second Half* and then apply the standard dark red shape fill (first option in the *Standard Colors* section).

h. Change the chart height to 4 inches and the chart width to 6.25 inches.

i. Use the Position button in the Arrange group to position the chart in the middle center of the page with square text wrapping.

2. Save the document with the name **U2-SalesChart**.

3. Print **U2-SalesChart**.

4. With the chart selected, display the Excel worksheet and then edit the data in the worksheet by changing the following:

a. Change the amount in cell C2 from *$285,450* to *$302,500*.

b. Change the amount in cell C4 from *$180,210* to *$190,150*.

5. Save, print, and then close **U2-SalesChart**.

Assessment 4

Create and Format a Pie Chart

1. At a blank document, use the data in Figure U2.2 to create a pie chart with the following specifications:

a. Apply the Layout 6 quick layout.

b. Apply the Style 3 chart style.

c. Change the chart title to *District Expenditures*.

d. Move the legend to the left side of the chart.

e. Select the chart area, apply the Gold, Accent 4, Lighter 80% shape fill (eighth column, second row in the *Theme Colors* section), and then apply the Glow: 11 point; Gray, Accent color 3 glow shape effect (third column, third row in the *Glow Variations* section).

f. Select the legend and apply the Blue color shape outline (eighth option in the *Standard Colors* section).

g. Move the data labels to the inside ends of the pie pieces.

h. Select the legend and center it between the left edge of the chart border and the pie.

i. Use the Position button to center the chart at the top of the page with square text wrapping.

2. Save the document with the name **U2-ExpendChart**.

3. Print and then close **U2-ExpendChart**.

Figure U2.2 Assessment 4

	Percentage
Basic Education	42%
Special Needs	20%
Support Services	19%
Vocational	11%
Compensatory	8%

Assessment **Merge and Print Letters**

5

1. Look at the information shown in Figure U2.3 and Figure U2.4. Use the Mail Merge feature to prepare six letters using the information shown in the figures. When creating the letter main document, open **SoundLtrhd** and then save it with the name **U2-SoundMD**. (Change the punctuation in the greeting line from a comma to a colon.) Create the data source file with the text shown in Figure U2.3 and name the file **U2-SoundDS**. (When creating the data source, customize the columns to accommodate the text in the figure.)
2. Type the text in the main document as shown in Figure U2.4. Insert the *Title* and *Last_Name* fields in the last paragraph as indicated.
3. Merge the document with the **U2-SoundDS** data source file.
4. Save the merged letters document and name it **U2-SoundLtrs**. Print and then close the document.
5. Save and then close the main document.

Assessment **Merge and Print Envelopes**

6

1. Use the Mail Merge feature to prepare Size 10 envelopes for the letters created in Assessment 5.
2. Specify **U2-SoundDS** as the data source document.
3. Save the merged envelopes document and name the document **U2-SoundEnvs**.
4. Print and then close **U2-SoundEnvs**.
5. Save the envelope main document with the name **U2-SoundEnvMD** and then close the document.

Figure U2.3 Assessment 5

Mr. Antonio Mercado
3241 Court G
Tampa, FL 33623

Ms. Kristina Vukovich
1120 South Monroe
Tampa, FL 33655

Ms. Alexandria Remick
909 Wheeler South
Tampa, FL 33620

Mr. Minh Vu
9302 Lawndale Southwest
Tampa, FL 33623

Mr. Curtis Iverson
10139 93rd Court South
Tampa, FL 33654

Ms. Holly Bernard
8904 Emerson Road
Tampa, FL 33620

December 14, 2021

«AddressBlock»

«GreetingLine»

Sound Medical is switching hospital care in Tampa to Bayshore Hospital beginning January 1, 2022. As mentioned in last month's letter, Bayshore Hospital was selected because it meets our requirements for high-quality, patient-centered care that is also affordable and accessible. Our physicians look forward to caring for you in this new environment.

Over the past month, staff members at Sound Medical have been working to make this transition as smooth as possible. Surgeries planned after January 1 are being scheduled at Bayshore Hospital. Mothers delivering babies after January 1 are receiving information about delivery room tours and prenatal classes available at Bayshore Hospital. Your Sound Medical doctor will have privileges at Bayshore Hospital and will continue to care for you if you need to be hospitalized.

You are a very important part of our patient family, «Title» «Last_Name», and we hope this information is helpful. If you have any additional questions or concerns, please call our health coordinator at (813) 555-9886 between 8:00 a.m. and 4:30 p.m.

Sincerely,

Jody Tiemann
District Administrator

XX
U2-SoundMD

Assessment 7

Create and Insert Custom Building Blocks

1. Using the Open dialog box in Word, open the template **CPTemplate** and then save it as a template with the name **U2-CPTemplate**.
2. This template contains three custom building blocks for Capital Properties. Add two more custom building blocks with the following specifications:
   a. Select the heading *Attorney's Fees* and the paragraph of text below the heading and then save the selected text in a custom building block in the Quick Part gallery with the name *Fees*.
   b. Select the image (the horizontal line and house with *Est. 1990*) and then save the image as a custom building block in the Footer gallery with the name *CPFooter*.
3. Select and then delete the entire document.
4. Save and then close **U2-CPTemplate**.
5. Use File Explorer to open a blank document based on **U2-CPTemplate**.
6. Build a real estate agreement by completing the following steps:
   a. Insert the *CPHeader* building block located in the Header gallery. Close the Header pane.
   b. Insert the *CPFooter* building block located in the Footer gallery. Close the Footer pane.
   c. Insert the *REAgreement* building block located in the Quick Part gallery.
7. Save the document and name it **U2-CPAgreement**.
8. Print and then close **U2-CPAgreement**.
9. Use File Explorer to open a blank document based on **U2-CPTemplate**.
10. Build a lease agreement by completing the following steps:
    a. Insert the *CPHeader* building block located in the Header gallery. Close the Header pane.
    b. Insert the *CPFooter* building block located in the Footer gallery. Close the Footer pane.
    c. Insert the *LeaseAgreement* building block located in the Quick Part gallery.
    d. Move the insertion point to the beginning of the heading *Use of Premises* and then insert the *Fees* building block in the Quick Part gallery. (If necessary, press the Enter key to start a new paragraph at the *Use of Premises* heading.)
11. Save the document and name it **U2-CPLease**.
12. Print and then close **U2-CPLease**.

Assessment 8

Insert Comments and Track Changes in an Online Shopping Report

1. Open **OnlineShop** and then save it with the name **U2-OnlineShop**.
2. Move the insertion point to end of the first paragraph in the report and then insert a comment and type the following comment text: Include the source where you found this definition.
3. Move the insertion point to the end of the paragraph in the *Online Shopping Venues* section and then insert a comment and type the following comment text: Include at least two of the most popular online shopping stores.
4. Click the *Display for Review* option box arrow and then click *All Markup* at the drop-down list, if necessary.
5. Turn on Track Changes and then make the following changes:
   a. Delete the comma and the words *and most are eliminating paper tickets altogether*, which display at the end of the last sentence in the second paragraph. (Do not delete the period that ends the sentence.)
   b. Edit the heading *Advantages of Online Shopping* so it displays as *Online Shopping Advantages*.

    c. Apply bold formatting to the first sentence of each bulleted paragraph on the first page.

    d. Turn off Track Changes.

6. Display the Word Options dialog box with *General* selected and then type Trudy Holmquist as the user name and TH as the user initials. (Make sure you insert a check mark in the *Always use these values regardless of sign in to Office* check box.)

7. Turn on Track Changes and then make the following changes:

    a. Delete the words *the following* in the first paragraph in the *Online Shopping Advantages* section.

    b. Type the following bulleted text between the third and fourth bulleted paragraphs on the second page: Keep thorough records of all transactions.

    c. Turn off Track Changes.

8. Print the document with markups.

9. Display the Word Options dialog box with *General* selected and then change the user name back to the original name and the initials back to the original initials. (Remove the check mark from the *Always use these values regardless of sign in to Office* check box.)

10. Accept all the changes in the document *except* reject the change deleting the comma and the text *and most are eliminating paper tickets altogether*. (Leave the comments in the document.)

11. Save, print, and then close **U2-OnlineShop**.

Assessment 9

Restrict Formatting in a Report

1. Open **CompPioneers** and then save it with the name **U2-CompPioneers**.

2. Display the Restrict Editing task pane and then restrict formatting to the Heading 1 and Heading 2 styles. (At the message that displays asking if you want to remove formatting or styles that are not allowed, click No.)

3. Enforce the protection and include the password *report*.

4. Click the <u>Available styles</u> hyperlink in the Restrict Editing task pane.

5. Apply the Heading 1 style to the title of the report (*PIONEERS OF COMPUTING*) and apply the Heading 2 style to the two headings in the report (*Konrad Zuse* and *William Hewlett and David Packard*).

6. Close the Styles task pane.

7. Close the Restrict Editing task pane.

8. Save, print, and then close **U2-CompPioneers**.

Writing Activities

Activity

1

Create Building Blocks and Compose a Letter

You are the executive assistant to the vice president of Clearline Manufacturing. You are responsible for preparing company documents and decide to create building blocks to increase the efficiency of and consistency in the documents. Press Ctrl + N to open a blank document and then save the document as a template named **U2-CMTemplate** in your WL2U2 folder. Create the following building blocks in the template:

- Create a letterhead that includes the company name and any other enhancements to improve the appearance. Save the letterhead as a building block in the Header gallery.

- Create a building block footer that inserts the company address and telephone number. (You determine the address and telephone number.) Include a visual element in the footer, such as a border. Save the footer building block in the Footer gallery.

- You send documents to the board of directors and decide to include the board members' names and addresses as building blocks. Save each board member's name and address as a building block in the Quick Part gallery.

Ms. Nancy Logan
12301 132nd Avenue East
Warminster, PA 18974

Mr. Dion Jarvis
567 Federal Street
Philadelphia, PA 19093

Dr. Austin Svoboda
9823 South 112th Street
Norristown, PA 18974

- Create a complimentary close building block that includes *Sincerely yours,* your name, and the title *Executive Assistant*. Save the building block in the Quick Part gallery.

Delete the contents of **U2-CMTemplate** and then save the template. (This saves the building blocks you created in the template.)

At a blank document, write the body of a letter to a member of the board of directors and include at least the following information:

- Explain that the director of the Human Resources Department has created a new employee handbook and that it will be made available to all new employees. Also mention that the attorney for Clearline Manufacturing has reviewed the handbook and approved its content.

- Open **CMHandbook** and then use the headings to summarize the contents of the handbook in a paragraph in the letter. Explain in the letter that a draft of the handbook is enclosed.

- Include any additional information you feel the directors may want to know.

Save the body of the letter as a separate document named **U2-CMLtr** and then close **U2-CMLtr**. Use File Explorer to open a blank document based on **U2-CMTemplate** and then create a letter to Nancy Logan with the following specifications:

- Insert the letterhead building block you created for Clearline Manufacturing.
- Insert the footer building block.
- Insert the building block containing Nancy Logan's name and address.
- Insert into the document the file named **U2-CMLtr**.

- Insert the complimentary close building block.
- Insert any other text or make any changes to complete the letter.

Save the completed letter and name it **U2-CMLtrNL**. Print and then close the letter. Complete similar steps to create a letter to Dion Jarvis. Save the letter and name it **U2-CMLtrDJ**. Print and then close the letter. Complete similar steps to create a letter to Austin Svoboda. Save the letter and name it **U2-CMLtrAS**. Print and then close the letter.

Activity 2

Create a Slogan Building Block

You decide to create a building block for the company slogan and save it in **U2-CMTemplate**. Open **U2-CMTemplate** from your WL2U2 folder. In the template, create a text box with the slogan *Where innovation and production come together.* inside the text box. Enhance the appearance of the text box by applying formatting similar to that applied to the company letterhead. After creating the text box, select it and then save it in the Text Box gallery with the name **CMSlogan**. After saving the text box as a building block, delete the text box and then save and close **U2-CMTemplate**. Use File Explorer to open a document based on **U2-CMTemplate**. Insert the letterhead header building block and the footer building block you created in Activity 1 and then insert the text box building block you created in this activity. Save the document and name it **U2-CMDocument**. Print and then close **U2-CMDocument**.

Internet Research

Create a Population Chart

Use a search engine to determine the population of the country in which you currently live for the years 1970, 1980, 1990, 2000, and 2010. Create a line chart with the information you find. Apply formatting to the chart to make the data easy to interpret and to improve the visual interest of the chart.

Save the document and name it **U2-Population**. Print and then close **U2-Population**.

Job Study

Format a Guidelines Report

As a staff member of a computer e-tailer, you are required to maintain cutting-edge technology skills, including being well versed in the use of new software applications, such as those in the Microsoft Office suite. Recently, your supervisor asked you to develop and distribute a set of strategies for reading technical and computer manuals that staff members will use as they learn new applications. Use the concepts and techniques you learned in this textbook to edit the guidelines report as follows:

1. Open **Strategies** and then save it with the name **U2-Strategies**.
2. Turn on Track Changes and then make the following changes:
   a. Change all the occurrences of *computer manuals* to *technical and computer manuals*.
   b. Format the document with appropriate heading styles.
   c. Turn off Track Changes.
   d. Insert at least two comments about the content and/or formatting of the document.
   e. Print the list of markups.
   f. Accept all the Tracked Changes.
3. Insert a table of contents.
4. Number the pages in the document.
5. Insert a cover page.
6. Save, print, and then close **U2-Strategies**.